# Academia in Anarchy

# ACADEMIA
# IN
# ANARCHY

*An Economic Diagnosis*

James M. Buchanan
& Nicos E. Devletoglou

BASIC BOOKS, INC., PUBLISHERS

NEW YORK    LONDON

TO

*The Taxpayer*

Intimidation and threats remain outlaw weapons in a free society. A fundamental governing principle of any great university is that the rule of reason and not the rule of force prevails. Whoever rejects that principle forfeits his right to be a member of the academic community. The university administrator who fails to uphold that principle jeopardizes one of the central pillars of his institution and weakens the very foundation of American education.

RICHARD M. NIXON

# Preface

Almost everyone, whether inside or outside the university, has his own description of what is happening to this once-stable institution of society. There are also as many prescriptions as to what should be done to improve things as there are men who make them. If anything, the chaos in discussion exceeds that in the events discussed. What seems to be needed most at this point is less talk from the top of soft heads and more thought in hard heads. There can be little doubt that we should stop making proposals for reform before we understand what we are observing. Prescription follows, it does not precede, explanation. And the feature most wanting is an explanation of the turmoil. To provide explanatory visions is the function of theory in all its applications. We certainly need not shun theory here.

Alone among the social sciences, economics has a general theory. It starts with a model of behavior which explains many aspects of the modern world, although by no means all. Should we not expect an economic vision of academia to be helpful? This book is an application of simple economic theory to the university chaos that is developing everywhere.

# Preface

We are professional economists and we hold permanent positions on university faculties. The first equips us to apply economic reasoning; the second equips us to apply this reasoning to the university. A third quality equips us to apply economics directly to our increasingly chaotic environment. We have both been where the "action" is. Both of us have held visiting and permanent positions on two of the world's more distinguished hot spots, the University of California and the London School of Economics.

Buchanan was a permanent member of the faculty of the University of California, Los Angeles. He resigned his post during the academic year 1968–1969. He experienced the bombing of the economics department's offices in November, 1968. In the spring of 1967, Buchanan was Visiting Professor at the London School of Economics, just after the initial series of disruptions in March of that year.

Devletoglou was Visiting Professor at the University of California, Los Angeles, during the winter and spring of 1969. He is a permanent member of the faculty of the London School of Economics. He took an active interest in the episodic events at the School in 1967 and 1968, especially in the fall of 1968, when the pattern of intimidation by activist minority "students" crystallized.

Both of us observed, jointly and at first-hand, the campus shock that followed the assassination of two Black Panther students during a UCLA "students' discussion" in January, 1969, an event that took place within a stone's throw of our own offices. We also watched in shame the groveling of the UCLA administrative authorities before the militant threats in late May, 1969. Our combined personal experience, and especially that described by events at the University of California during the time this book was being written, necessarily influences our discussion of university turmoil despite efforts on our part to insure that the analysis retains general applicability. This limitation is, we trust, offset by the experience itself which guarantees that we do not write from ignorance.

We do write from indignation. We sense acutely the tragedy that is occurring before our very eyes, a tragedy in which the absurd behavior of "liberal" academic reformers allows a handful of revolutionary terrorists to undo the heritage of centuries. The situation on campuses throughout the world becomes critical as terrorist tactics and endless varieties of intellectual and physical vandalism become more and more fashionable.

But we also write from hope. The application of elementary economic theory provides a new glimpse of what is happening in academia. We make no claim that our diagnosis is comprehensive nor that our treatment is, in any sense, encyclopedic. We seek only to show why terror has been so effective in our midst, why it has succeeded in systematically ravaging the fruits of years of intellectual effort and achievement in our universities. Foul winds, no doubt, are blowing. What the economist's approach yields is some explanation of why the universities' walls are made of straw—together with the promise of transforming them into walls of brick.

*Los Angeles / January, 1970*                    J.M.B. / N.E.D.

# Acknowledgments

The urgency of the issues dictated that we write this book in haste. Many scholars have generally influenced our thinking and have indirectly contributed to our approach to the university. Prominent among them are Professors Armen A. Alchian and Gordon Tullock, who also read the first draft of the manuscript in its entirety and made helpful suggestions for revision.

We owe each other, and the readers, some acknowledgment as to our separate shares in the book. The whole book is a joint product, but some initial assignment of work was necessary. Buchanan wrote the first drafts of Chapters 3, 4, and 6. Devletoglou assumed first responsibility for Chapters 2, 5, and 7. Chapters 1 and 8 were genuinely joint products at all stages.

We should also express our appreciation to Mrs. Carmela von Bawey for her assistance at various stages of the manuscript. Her willingness to remain cheerful while working to deadlines helped to make feverish times also pleasant ones.

# Contents

# PART ONE

# Chapter 1

# *Setting the Scene*

Many universities are in chaos. Unrepresentative but well-organized groups of students use their precious time and other people's wealth to participate in "sit-ins" or "invasions," to foment trouble, and deliberately to upset the learning process. Wanton physical destruction of university property proceeds apace, with losses mounting into the tens of millions. What is worse, these students pursue objectives unrelated to the purposes and standards upon which the academic world is based, objectives which, if achieved, may inflict incalculable losses on modern society. Famous universities and their revolting students find themselves hanging on the ropes, as it were, seriously battered and waiting in anguish for the bell to ring and the vacation period to save one from the other. The spectacle is a painful one. And the general public is rightly becoming indignant.

The need to take a fresh look at the basic structure and functions of contemporary university life is urgently real.

# Scarcity in Education

*First-day Economics and the University Chaos*

The student protest movement is to a large extent an expression of the social and political extremism with which we have increasingly come to live everywhere else in society. Much of it flows from the rapidly spreading taste for (and rising returns in) terror and myth-making, best developed among those addicted to a disregard of lawful conventions as a means of protest against the intrinsic nature of constitutional government. No society, however, whether democratic or not, can tolerate such practices without degenerating into anarchy. Reluctant to face this simple fact, people have instead sought to interpret and understand the university chaos as an outgrowth of burning social and political issues.

It may be, however, that the viability of trespass and threat of violence in many universities today is better understood as the result of the manner in which university education is organized and financed. Why does the modern protest have its outcroppings in the university setting? Is it possible to explain this largely by the structure of the institutions themselves?

4

## Setting the Scene

The purpose of this book is to inquire along these lines with the help of the simplest tools of economic analysis available. An added incentive for this inquiry is the prospect that, given time, today's responding reformers may well prove equally, if not more dangerous than their revolutionary counterparts. Too sensitive to sporadic acts of social and political vandalism, they often set in motion processes that tend to change things bit by bit. The resulting differences are seldom apparent to everyone at once; yet at some stage most of us emerge conscious of certain singularly unattractive features of the world in which we then must live. One has only to glance at university life today to see how rapidly it has been deteriorating, though hardly ever in a pattern which could be said to have resulted from revolution at any particular moment.

No economist worth his salt can look at the university world today without being forced to apply elementary economic theory in an effort to explain and to understand. Almost alone among social scientists, the economist brings with him a model of human behavior which allows predictions about human action. He looks first at the economic rewards and punishments that the institutions place before human choice-makers. The economist does not, of course, claim that all men behave as his model predicts. And, especially, he does not presume that students and scholars motivated by the pursuit of knowledge are solely, or primarily, responsive to economic pressures.

Nonetheless, the economist faces squarely up to the fact that *university education is not a free good*. It does not

5

abound in nature, and considerable scarcity value attaches to it. Resources that could be used to produce other things that are valued by men and women have to be employed to produce university education. Education is, in other words, an *economic* good. For this reason, the economic aspects of its demand and its supply cannot be wholly neglected. But if people will so curiously insist on arguing that university education is a free good, those who demand, supply, and finance it will begin to act as if it were, in fact, free! Increasing numbers of students will demand more and more university places, better and better physical facilities, and increasingly attentive devotion to their "special needs." Regardless of the supply of faculties and facilities, demands will invariably be excessive. When nominal (below cost) or zero prices are fixed on so expensive a good, it becomes inevitable that nonprice rationing, in some form or other, must be adopted. In addition, suppliers become increasingly immune to consumer desires, being allowed, as it were, to "give away" an expensive good for which demand is excessive. Worse still, the product predictably deteriorates as suppliers begin to take on the arrogance of despots. But suppliers are not donors. They do not personally bear the costs of charity. Again, the delusion that university education is a free good leads to disregard both for cost reduction and for efficiency in large or small matters.

This is first-day economics. Yet its truth is widely denied, and institutions reflect this denial. Implicit in much of the 1967–1969 discussion about the desirability of tuition charges in California was the assumption that higher education "should be" treated as a "free good," even when its costs are recognized. It was argued that students (or their parents) "should not" be charged for university education. But, if not directly charged, who "should" pay? If resources are to be given up, whose resources are these to be? The answer too often given is some vague and mystical reference to the state, the public purse, without any direct relationship to the individual as taxpayer.

Today in much of higher education governments alone impose the ultimate economic constraints. Education can scarcely be treated as if it were free in governmental budgets. For this, quite simply, would mean a budgeted total of zero. Of course, funds are scarce, and education stands in line for its share of society's resources—even if awarded high priority. This ultimate scarcity of funds coupled with free-floating suppliers and unsatisfied demanders, both of whom deny the economic essence of the product, creates the institutional patterns we observe. Faculty pay scales are often fixed and applied uniformly with little or no regard for economic factors. Inferior staff is treated indistinguishably from superior staff. The latter seek additional employment outside the university setting, take a less direct interest in university life, and prefer to measure their productivity by their research or publication efforts. Consequently, inferior staff tend to carry the university's day-to-day operations, and rationing criteria (that is, basic fixing of entry-study-graduation standards) are systematically determined by less and less qualified persons.

## University Education: A Unique Industry

University education, when examined through economists' eyes, assumes characteristics of a unique industry. This is because: (1) those who consume its product do not purchase it; (2) those who produce it do not sell it; and (3) those who finance it do not control it. Is it surprising that the orderly processes that seem to characterize standard commercial dealings seem to break down in universities?

What should be predicted to happen when those who consume a good directly are not required to purchase or to pay for this good? Is it not inevitable that demand will tend to exceed supply? Can there ever be a sufficient number of university places to meet all demands for places? Will the quality of product ever be such as to please those who need not pay for quality improvements? Does not the necessity of rationing the available supply of university educational services become obvious?

Furthermore, what can be said about a good which is produced by those who do not sell it? University education is directly produced by faculties and administrators. They do not sell the services they perform to those who consume them. Hence, is there any difficulty in making the elementary prediction that few, if any, attempts will be made to satisfy directly the demands of consumers? Without the standard test of consumer acceptance that an effectively free market forces on producers, there is no feedback on the

8

latter's behavior. Is there any wonder that faculties offer the sort of product they themselves derive most pleasure in supplying—in turn, a product which need not meet the desires of those for whom it is produced?

Finally, what about those who finance the output, the taxpayers (or private donors), who through governmental (or charitable) processes must ultimately sacrifice the economic resources which university education requires? If the institutions are such as to prevent their control over product quality, how can their continued financial support be expected? Who is so otherworldly as to invest resources in a product that is deliberately shrouded in veils of mystery and propaganda as to its ultimate value?

The questions raised here amount to little more than the consistent turning of a few analytical cranks known to every professional economist. Yet they will surely arouse passionate opposition. Many advocates for many positions will emerge to deny the essential verities that the economist expounds, even when all efforts at qualifying these are made. As the chaos mounts, however, and as the reformers' feeble but sometimes dangerous responses to revolutionary pressures continue, as the taxpayers rise in anger, perhaps the time will come when the economist's pedestrian explanations will command respect. This respect for and understanding of the economics of university chaos may lead to suggestions for constructive rather than destructive reform. Perhaps most importantly, an understanding of elementary economics produces an appreciation of the simple truth that the institutions within which men make choices can themselves modify these choices. This truth un-aided can do much.

# Education as a One-Way "Trip"

Economists busy themselves with measuring rates of return to investment in schooling at all levels. This economics of education is fashionable territory. The data are drained dry for every conceivable test that modern computers make so tempting to those whom thought may trouble. Now and again faint protest is heard. Can education properly be treated as a mere input in the production of incomes, as measured by economists?

But if education is not investment, what is it? Is education-as-consumption a feasible alternative? If education is not like machinery, is it then like apples? If not like either, what can economists do? Until and unless we can answer this elementary question, we shall get confused at the outset. We should hold off trying to apply elementary economics, as promised, until we can at least identify the thing to which it is being applied.

## Professional Training

Before essaying a specific answer, let us clear the decks. Mixed up with what we call university education is professional training of all sorts. Here the economics is easy at the conceptual level. We are talking about productive input and investment; professional training is precisely like machinery. Outlay, whether made directly by the student or his family or indirectly by the taxpayer through the governmental process, represents capital investment. This is aimed at enhancing the income-producing power of the human agent, with income being measured strictly by production of value in the nation's marketplace. The efficiency norms are familiar. Why? Because both for the individual as investor and for the community, professional training is not "terra incognita." Therefore, investment is simply carried to the point at which the extra return equals the extra cost, with care being taken to measure properly. If university education were limited to professional training the chaos that we observe might be nonexistent. Relative calm prevails in those areas of university life that are strictly professional—students here know what they are after. And to know what one wants is to have half of one's problems solved. Also, professional training, as such, is much more likely to be sold at a price.

## Education as Leisure

There is also some specific consumption mixed up with the package that we call university education. In this case, we are talking about output that is defined readily as "an interesting passing of the time." No end objectives are in view and none are even contemplated. Education in this vision, which is omnipresent, is merely a means of getting through difficult years, and is not one whit different from afternoon trips to the movies for the children. It is aimed at making the users, the students, happy. If this were all there is to university education, again the economic analysis would be simple and the norms for improvement relatively easy to specify. If the aim is to make students happy, then why not organize our institutions with nothing but this in view? Relative calm would prevail, and who prefers chaos when it can be avoided? This is why we observe, in fact, that those areas of university life where this aspect of the educational process takes precedence are also tranquil islands in the storm. Riots rarely occur at lecture series produced primarily for the "little old ladies" who live near the campuses.

## Education as a Psychedelic Game

If we eliminate professional training and the pleasant passing of time as end objectives, we are left with the essence of university education. We are face to face with the real problem in university life today—the generally unanswered question, What is education to those who consume it? The chaos that we see arises because education is something more than investment and consumption, something which is at the same time both and neither.

We can take advantage of modern idiom here. As our earlier heading suggests, education is a one-way "trip." It resembles a psychedelic transformation minus the return to the launching pad. The product is a process, a happening through time, to which the student submits in the knowledge that he will become and remain sensorily different from what he is. Because outcomes remain unknown and unpredictable, elements of a game are involved here, a game played against or with life itself. The student migrates to "the undiscover'd country" from which "no traveller returns." But who can rationally exercise choice over such a process? Who can logically evaluate the results? If the student knows the outcome there is no problem. Here professional training is the model. The student knows what he will be able to do when he completes his course of study. But there is no "education" in this. The genuine educational process does not "train." It "transforms." It provides the student with a different and new way of looking at the world, a new vision that is akin to that produced by religious conversion or an LSD trip. It does this not suddenly but over a time-constrained sequence. The student is neither Saint Paul on the road to Damascus nor the hippie who sees the cube-caused colors in his pad. But his vision is changed—and, unlike the hippie, permanently so, as he moves through the higher learning experience. With university education, then, all prospective consumers find themselves in the curious situation of committing themselves in favor of a product they do not know. University education is like a blind date after all.

*The University Student as Child-Man*

We must accept the university student as a child-man. The child is one "for whom choices are made"; The man is "one who makes choices." The student has a foot in both worlds. He is both child and man, and this ambivalence cannot be overlooked if we are to understand what we see. Were he child alone, we could naturally drop all reference to choice. Parents choose for children and parental wisdom is presumably sufficient to generate broadly acceptable patterns of selection. Parents, as buyers of education, supplemented as required by taxpayers who share the public-goods benefits of common schooling, know what they want and they can evaluate alternative processes with some sophistication.

To an extent, parents or friends can do the same for the university child. University-trained parents and friends, having gone through the transformation that the university experience provides, can choose rationally among alternative processes offered. They can probably sense, too, the inefficiency in monolithic institutions when competition is absent. But we live in times of the education, as well as the population, explosion. The great majority of American and European university children have access to sources who know little more about the university experience than they do themselves. Parents or friends who have no knowledge of the relevant mysteries can hardly be expected to make rational choices as to these divines. Add to this the permissiveness that is preached by psychologists, and increasingly accepted by society, and the result is the university child-man, launched into a world which he cannot possibly know or understand—a world almost Delphic in its intricacy, strange, enchanted, forbidding, challenging, and absolutely necessary. The child "plays" man and is expected to choose, to exert his own being, to select his own options among processes of transformation that must embody almost maximum uncertainties.

Is it not predictable that excessive power should have been transferred to the academicians, those "experts" who maintain the citadels of learning, the university faculties and administrators who stand willing, perhaps eager, to pronounce to all concerned what process of education is "good" for each and every one? Is it not predictable, too, that the child-becoming-man student should rebel against the enforced diet that is offered to him? Besides, "standing up" a blind date can even be fun.

As will be seen in subsequent chapters, the application of the simplest economic tools to these and other unpleasant facts around us will go a long way to explain university chaos today. At the same time, we should have proceeded in default had we not recognized, and explicitly, at the outset, the peculiar nature of the transformation process that university education represents.

*Callias, I said, if your sons had been colts or calves, we should have had no difficulty in finding and engaging a trainer to perfect their natural qualities, and this trainer would have been some sort of horse dealer or agriculturalist. But seeing that they are human beings, whom do you intend to get as their instructor? Who is the expert in perfecting the human and social qualities? I assume from the fact of your having sons that you must have considered the question. Is there such a person or not?*
*Certainly, said he.*

*Who is he, and where does he come from? said I, and what does he charge?*

*Evenus of Paros, Socrates, said he, and his fee is five minas.*

*I felt that Evenus was to be congratulated if he really was a master of this art and taught it at such a moderate fee. I should certainly plume myself and give myself airs if I understood these things, but in fact, gentlemen, I do not.*

Socrates' Defense (Plato, *Apologia*)

# Chapter 2

# *Students: Consumers Who Do Not Buy*

Most high school graduates feel they must "go on" these days. Despite the ambiguities or the difficulties which await them—even the physical and psychological dangers inherent in the turmoil of many universities today—their minds are made up. They are not familiar with the transformation process they seek for themselves. University education is nonetheless the only thing that matters. For better or worse, the majority feel no qualms about taking any of the necessary leaps. The goodness of the course becomes undeniable to them, and its worth must not, cannot be questioned. Its pursuit is sacred. Everything else, including the many other opportunities foregone, becomes subservient to it. In endless streams, the faithful massively converge toward every campus in the nation year after year.

## Congestion and/or Rationing

Translated into economics, the demand for the services of college and university education has increased since the World War II and is still increasing dramatically. From 1.5 million in 1940, United States university-college enrollment swelled to 5.5 million by 1965. The number of students entering universities and colleges doubled over the decade extending from the late 1950's to the late 1960's. A threefold increase in student numbers took place in the United Kingdom between 1947 and 1965.

In the case of an ordinary product, an increase in demand generates pressure on prices. Prices rise so as to limit demands to available supplies. Prices serve as the balancing device which acts to bring demand and supply into equality. But what may be predicted when, despite the increased demand, prices are not allowed to rise? What will be the response when the services sought are known to be *freely* supplied? Each potential demander will expect to satisfy his fancy without paying the cost explicitly, although he will be paying something (indeed a considerable amount) implicitly through his sacrifice of foregone earnings. Adequate supplies to meet all demands at zero prices are simply not available, even in a land of relative plenty, such as the United States or the United Kingdom. What is more, the

18

number of university places will certainly not meet the demands for these places at the levels of *quality* which existed before the quantum jump in demand.

There are two means of limiting demand in a situation where price is not allowed to rise. The first is to allow the available facilities to become congested. This amounts to permitting quality to fall with the increased pressure of demand on available supplies. This is the solution that we have generally adopted for our city streets. As the number of automobiles has increased, we have permitted congestion to become worse and worse. Experience should have long since indicated that mere expansion of pavements cannot alone accommodate traffic demands. Congestion can be predicted to be the general response when the increased demands are for impersonal physical facilities.

Congestion is much less likely to be allowed to develop, even in the absence of pricing, when the demands are for personal services. Here resort to direct rationing is more probable. Some means, more or less arbitrary, will be found for separating actual consumers from potential consumers. It happens that the increased demand for the services of university education generates both responses. Physical facilities for students—rarely for staff—are allowed to become more and more congested. (One visit to the reading rooms at the London School of Economics library will convince any skeptic on this point.) Still more important, however, admissions policy will weed out some of the potential demanders for places. The rationing will be made primarily by restrictions on numbers of students rather than by the general quality deterioration which congestion represents.

There is no implication, however, that the quality of service maintained will reflect the preferences of students. Since they do not have to pay full value for services, what legitimate claims can students possibly have on the determination of university quality? The rationing process naturally enhances the discretionary power of those responsible for choosing among the many applicants and diminishes the power of those who are successful in securing admission.

When the inevitability of congestion or rationing (and in university education this amounts to rationing) is recognized, the whole concept of zero, or nominal (below cost) pricing, or "free tuition" comes into question. The only goods and services that may be reasonably provided at no prices to demanders are those that are "noneconomic." These are the so-called free goods, such as the air we breathe. They are normally found in so great abundance that their economic or scarcity value is naturally taken to be nil. Or they are such that, physically, it becomes impossible to separate one man's usage of them from another's. But university education is not at all of this sort. It is far from being a "free" good or service. It is an economic good—and a very expensive one at that. If university education should ever become something that everyone could freely consume, with no scarcity value attached to it at all, paradise lost would have at last been regained. We could all then become permanent scholars, discoursing in the idyllic world of the dreamers. Unfortunately, scarcity is still endemic in university life. As everywhere else, in education more is wanted than it is possible to produce and supply. Higher education carries a price to someone somewhere along the line—whether we want to call it a price or not. In addition, the funds that most governments are either able or willing to make available are strictly limited.

Recognizing this, what can "free tuition" mean? University education can, at best, be "free" only in the sense that a predetermined (and limited) number of university places are made available to certain students. But who are the lucky ones to be? This is a central question, and a source of much unrest. The tradition of zero or nominal tuition charges prevents universities from using the single most effective device in bringing about some equilibrium between the demand and the existing supply of university education. Can university authorities, and the public generally, continue to ignore the simple facts? How can informed argument proceed on the assumption that university education is best treated "as if" it were genuinely a free good? It seems clear that the whole question of tuition charges must be rationally discussed.

## What Is Free Tuition?

Free tuition is a strange public subsidy. In the production of university education, where those who produce do not sell their services, and those who own the facility do not control it, free tuition completes the curious circle. Those who consume the product do not have to buy it. This fundamental peculiarity apart, the characteristics of free tuition are akin to those generally associated with public subsidies. Free tuition is squarely based on the government's (and presumably a majority's) conviction that individuals will not, on their own, purchase a socially preferred amount of university education.

As with any other system of public subsidies, however, we may at once ask: Why should such and such a group in the community be subsidized and not others? Exactly what fortunate members of the group should be singled out as the direct recipients of the community's largesse? Or, to what extent and in what manner should such a gift be made? Considering these questions as a whole, two simple points must be made. Under *any* scheme of free tuition a highly subjective apparatus is invariably necessary to perform the requisite rationing of university places. Second, by the very fact of this self-imposed selectivity, free tuition is bound to attract suspicion to itself. Can zero tuition, or any particular level of charges below cost, be compatible with optimal schemes for rationing scarce university facilities? Or, can any general principles be laid down at all? Should not the great advantages of pricing be utilized, at least to some degree, under almost any rationing criteria and regardless of the particular social objectives? What is the effect of free tuition on those whom it is supposed to help? Those who are selected to be the final consumers of higher education do not have to pay explicitly for a certain part of what they get. But can this really be the matter of great "principle," as it is sometimes claimed? Why is free tuition such a "sacred cow"? Does Governor Reagan's proposal for charging tuition in California prove that he is out to destroy the institutions of higher learning? And why have academicians in California state universities and colleges so strongly resisted efforts to introduce even nominal tuition charges?

# The Deception of Free Tuition

Free tuition singles out a particular group to receive a particular subsidy in a particular form. So pronounced a selectivity might be expected to reflect certain truths that are so clear or so obvious that one should hardly bother to question them. Unfortunately, this is not the case. In fact, this extraordinary selectivity leaves open an uncomfortably large number of questions. This is all the more disturbing because very substantial community resources are involved here. They are resources for which many alternative uses certainly exist. Let us, therefore, take a closer look at the ambiguities involved.

To begin with, it is not clear whether *all* the students in the selected group should be subsidized to the *same* degree. If the objective is to distribute the community's scarce resources economically, there is good reason to argue that the extent of any subsidy should depend on such things as university performance (including a willingness to abide by ordinary rules of behavior), personal or family financial circumstances, field specialization, and so forth. In the second place, it is not clear why some of the students' expenses of higher education should be subsidized and not others. Consider the oddity that book fees, housing, laundry, or the more important item of opportunities for earnings foregone by the student, are not also included in the bill forwarded to the taxpayer! Finally, and perhaps most important, it is not evident that the subsidization of the student in higher education should take the particular *form* of direct financial support to the university as an institution. It could just as easily take the form of financial grants or loans made to the student directly. In other words, even if the principle of subsidization of students in higher education should be universally accepted, there is no implication that this should be done through the medium of zero or below cost tuition. It does not follow, that is to say, that universities must receive direct financial support from the government.

These are elementary doubts that an economist will raise when he takes a serious look at the existing programs of zero (state colleges) or nominal (private colleges) tuition schemes in existence.

## Is Free Tuition a Gift to the Gifted?

On a slightly more sophisticated level of analysis, it is not difficult to understand that much of today's loose philosophizing in favor of free tuition stems from a failure to distinguish two altogether different economic magnitudes: wealth and current earnings.

Measured in terms of current earnings, all prospective students are poor. Those whom we generally label as "rich" are those with the right parents. The students themselves are "poor" by any current-earnings measurement. But if measured in terms of wealth—the present value of future earnings—all students become rich relative to those who cannot qualify for admission to universities. In this latter and more meaningful sense, the subsidization of university students at the expense of the general taxpayer amounts to a transfer of wealth from the poor to the rich. This is, of course, the precise reverse of what ordinary standards of justice or equity have always suggested. Even at so broad a level of analysis, free tuition would seem to make the final distribution of income and wealth more, not less, unequal.

It is the perverse income-wealth transfer which most worries free tuition's staunchest advocates. And in order to salvage free tuition from the irrefutable logical assaults it attracts to itself, universities have embarked upon certain new programs. As we see in the next chapter, the emergence of chaos has been insured by these very programs. First, it came to be recognized that the whole program of free tuition subsidizes the young man with wealthy parents at the expense of the poor taxpayer in general. It finally dawned on university decision-makers that zero tuition naively redistributes wealth from the poor to the rich. Lower income groups provide the state schools with a smaller proportion of students than of taxes. In addition, it was discovered that the poor man's son could not generally meet the traditional admissions criteria based on accumulated academic records and test scores. Therefore, university faculties and administrators moved rapidly, in the late 1960's, to make exceptions so as to insure that "special" groups of poor students could gain admission. This whole procedure amounted to an attempt to preserve the free tuition concept by modifying the standard rationing scheme. Would it not have been more efficient to reduce the perverse distributive impact by installing a system of tuition charges based on scholarship loans or grants made *directly* to the students from poor families?

Any system, of course, which subsidizes students outright, whether through free tuition at state-supported universities or through grants (vouchers) made directly to the students themselves, will have some perverse distributive effects. This is because, in the final analysis, any such scheme will tend to favor the gifted rather than those who are not so fortunately endowed with the talents that equip them to secure the benefits of higher education.

Recognition of this simple point, as Harry Johnson has suggested, prompts arguments in support of student-loan schemes in opposition to student-grant systems.

# Free Tuition and Student Behavior

We need not argue the case for grants or loans here. Our purpose is limited to showing the effects of schemes which price educational services at zero or below cost levels, and the role of these schemes in creating at least part of the chaos that we witness in our major universities. One of the most important sources for this chaos stems directly from the attitudes that such policies generate in the student-consumer of higher education. Having successfully survived the initial rationing process, the student is offered a "free" service. Quite literally, he gets something for nothing. This has predictable behavioral effects. Specifically, the student will tend to treat the university, its faculty, and its facilities as if little or no scarcity value attaches to them. He will use these precisely as he would use a good that is, in effect, "free" in the economic sense of the term. There is no incentive for the student to avoid wastage of scarce resources. He has no conception, individually, that costs are involved at all. Is it to be wondered that he treats the whole university setting with disrespect or even with contempt?

The effects of free or nominal tuition schemes on student

behavior can perhaps best be seen by considering such behavior under alternative student-loan systems. In the latter the scarcity value of a university education would at least be brought home to the student. He, his parents, and his advisers would each be forced to think more seriously about opportunities foregone. They would, indeed, appreciate values sacrificed, even if not directly by the consumer himself. Still more important, the student might be induced to behave more rationally during his period of residence at the university itself. The sense that he is using his own resources, especially if these have been loaned to him, would tend to coax the student into making a better use of his precious university days. Above all, the property rights that students would so develop in their universities would contribute toward the elimination of the physical and intellectual vandalism we observe around us. The majority of students would have to consist of psychological monstrosities in order to be apathetic when *their* universities (financed by them and adequately catering to their revealed preferences) were invaded, ransacked, and closed down by a few of their fellows. In an atmosphere where it would have become possible to demonstrate that people on their own can meet a community need without government controls (other than those preserving the law of the land), the parasitic behavior of the few would not be likely to survive. Under such conditions, and with no second thoughts, the student-consumer might be more willing to defend his "property" from being vulgarized in the manner and style that seems common to universities today.

28

## Students: Consumers Who Do Not Buy

It is a well-known truth among economists that the free or below cost provision of a good will result in its inefficient use. This is illustrated by the attempt of the Russian government to give away bread. It was soon discovered that, when bread was made free, the peasants were feeding it to their cattle. University education is no different. And we should confidently predict that when it is made free, some consumers will use it inefficiently. Both in the groups of prospective and successful student-consumers, there will invariably be persons who place a value on university education lower than the cost of providing this education by whomever this cost is finally borne. If a person should place a value on university education above zero (net of the personal outlays that he must make), we may expect him to seek it regardless of the actual cost of providing this education to him. Suppose that a person places a net value of $100 on his admission to a university. Will he not in turn seek admission, even if the actual scarcity value of providing him a university place is $1000? The result is that a sizable proportion of university students, under any low tuition scheme, will be placing less value on what they are enjoying than they would place on other uses of these resources. It is not surprising, therefore, that such students will, even more than those discussed above, treat the university with disrespect and contempt.

## Is Free Tuition an Obstacle to Progress?

An additional effect of free tuition can now be seen in proper relief. By turning students into consumers who do not *buy*, free tuition stifles any tendency toward interuniversity competition. The allocation of scarce university resources consequently tends to become less efficient for this reason alone—and quite apart from those already mentioned. Under any scheme where students, themselves, are financed, rather than the universities, the producers of education would find it necessary to *compete* for students in order to obtain their resources. But what is happening instead? Thanks to widespread free or below cost tuition programs, the universities obtain finance directly from the government or from private donors and then proceed to make students compete for limited places. The student has to accept an educational offering which is determined by the highly subjective traditions built into the bureaucratic decision processes of universities. He is thus severely limited in his effective freedom to shop around in the expectation that competition will produce a product suited to his tastes and needs. No reason is readily apparent why taxpayers' money should be channelled to educational support indirectly through universities (which are then accountable to politicians), and not directly through consumers of university services (so that universities are answerable to them as customers).

## Students: Consumers Who Do Not Buy

High cost university education (combined with the government's commitment to finance so expensive a good from general tax revenues *and* the bias in favor of free or nominal tuition) has proved possible by forcing down costs at the expense of *all* those involved in university education. Why? The analytic sequence seems simple enough. As we shall argue in some detail in the next chapter, university staff is responsible for determining the nature of the process of rationing. Faculty and administration select the anointed few, and they even decide what to do with them. As a result of the government's interest, even necessity, in keeping costs within some limits, however, pay scales for university staff are often also artificially fixed. This further intensifies the usual effects of price control in leading to the deterioration of the quality of the product offered. Either inferior staff remains full-time at the universities to carry out their everyday operations, or better staff seeks additional income elsewhere, thereby taking a less direct interest in the affairs of the university. The indiscriminate treatment of better and worse staff built into the structure of higher education today further accelerates this process. More of those who by virtue of their inferiority enjoy "rents" (that is, surplus returns they could get nowhere else) remain full-time on the staff. Better qualified persons have more attractive alternatives and do not feel at all bound by any such "rents." They can command equal, if not higher, rewards elsewhere. Either way, as we see in Chapter 3, the basic fixing of university entry-study-graduation standards is more and more determined by the less and less qualified persons who remain in the universities. But the nature of the selection or rationing process can only suffer as it becomes progressively more personalized. And so does the process of education offered.

Not only, then, does the present system of "free" education lead to a process of rationing which is controlled by less and less qualified academics and administrators. In addition, it serves to increase the propensity of high school graduates to try to enter universities. But by so doing it expands further the excess demand for university places—popularizing the false impression that university education is free. As it is, university education is surrounded by a much undeserved aura of importance as an essential step to a better life ahead.

One basic conclusion is now apparent. The interposition of the government between the universities and their student-consumers has created a situation in which universities cannot meet demand and tap directly resources for satisfying student-consumer preferences. In order to get resources, universities have to compete with other tax-financed activities (armed forces, lower schools, welfare programs, and so forth). In the process, student-consumer demand is neglected, and the resulting student unrest provides the ingredients for the chaos we observe. An obvious contrast here would be a situation in which universities might be competitors for resources in the style of publishers or automobile manufacturers. Universities would then compete for students in order to obtain their finance, instead of obtaining their finance from the government and then making students compete for a limited number of places. They would then have to put their emphasis on satisfying their customers or explaining to them why they ought to be satisfied. In fact, if every university were so obliged to live by the verdicts which the community would express in terms of the use made of their goods and services, the education industry might cease to have many of today's reasons for disintegrating.

In this light, the "unbelievable" turmoil and dismal nonsense engulfing the contemporary university world becomes partially understandable. On balance, the elimination of this chaos may, by implication, require some shift toward greater interuniversity competition which would embody more usage of market-type adjustments. The mounting dependence on governmental financial support, as this has been translated into the institution of free tuition, may itself be one significant source of current unrest. To this extent, and regardless of objectives, the increasing dependence on governments may have wrought more harm than good.

*The residents in Watts, in short, subsidize the residents in Beverly Hills to attend the University of California. To advance a subsidy to students and not require repayment is to grant students a gift of wealth at the expense of those who do not attend college or who attend tuition-colleges and pay for themselves.*

Armen A. Alchian and William R. Allen, "What Price Zero Tuition?" *Michigan Quarterly Review* (October, 1968).

# Chapter 3

# *Faculties: Producers Who Do Not Sell*

It is never easy to subject personal interest to scientific examination. Since most economists hold university positions, it is not surprising that so few have applied their elementary analysis to their own institutions. We are no exceptions, and there is a sense of betrayal in this effort. We must imply that the never-never land of modern academia is little more than a glorious dream. Shattering illusions is devil's work, as Eugene O'Neill's *The Iceman Cometh* vividly recalls, and all the more so when the illusions are one's own. Would it were different, but events have forced upon us the necessity for rational rather than romantic understanding. Failing this, the "noble student" of the academic reformer's dream stands on the threshold of generating tragic results akin to those produced by Rousseau's "noble savage."

## The Automobile-Producing "Faculty"

Imagine an industry that produces an ordinary product, say automobiles. Imagine, too, that it is organized along the same lines as university education in, say, California. Suppose that automobiles are produced in institutions by "faculties," who then give them away to consumers. Assume further that the economic resources for the whole undertaking are provided by the taxpayers through governmental grants to suppliers, and that only nominal and indirect control is exercised over the whole operation. In Chapter 2, we have already discussed the effects of this pricing scheme on the behavior of the consumers—in our case, the students. In Chapter 4, we shall discuss the financing agent, the taxpayer, who pays but does not exercise direct control. In this chapter, we concentrate on faculties, or on university staff generally, including administrators. We consider their behavior as this is affected by the peculiar structure of the university. This is our most personal discussion, because, after all, we are examining our own behavior. But this, too, has advantages. Introspection properly tamed can be a helpful analytical device.

*Selection of Consumers*

Our selection of an ordinary industry is deliberate. Here we can make plausible predictions about behavior in the absence of romance. Imagine our "faculty," producing something like automobiles. At zero price, these are highly sought-after by consumers. To the producer, demands seem inexhaustible, and the number of demanders legion. By the nature of the problem that he confronts, the producer chooses which demanders to satisfy. He selects one set of customers from among many potential demanders. He discriminates. Rationing is forced upon him. And, as anyone who has suffered the abuse of petty bureaucrats knows, rationing embodies power of man over man. At this point, too, we should face another fact squarely. Individuals enjoy power. They relish opportunities to control the lives of others, and there are few exceptions to this generalization. Faced with what appears to be an almost limitless demand for whatever he may offer, the producer begins, all too naturally, to enjoy his role as chooser. Is it so strange that we should predict some loss of humility here? Is it not probable that the producing "faculty" member would begin to think himself omnipotent—or, indeed, to fashion himself as being in unique possession of the relevant criteria for good judgment?

The excess number of demanders, as already said, forces the producer to choose. He, therefore, discriminates along one dimension, that which delineates actual consumers from potential consumers. But he will also establish criteria for selection that reflect his *own* set of priorities. This is not to say that these will necessarily be based on narrowly defined self-interest. He may genuinely try to arrive at "reasonable" standards of discrimination. He may give away automobiles only to those who are most able to drive. Discriminating on some criterion of *ability* seems sensible enough. Or, of course, he may do just the opposite. He may give away automobiles only to those who have not had *access* to such goods before. Is discriminating on some grounds of charity sensible, too? It depends. The central point is that *he* must choose, and that his choice will be influenced by *his own* priorities.

Naturally, discrimination implies that some potential consumers remain unsatisfied. That is to say, some will have to be discriminated against. Unless the potential consumers should somehow separate themselves into "natural" groups that are roughly similar to those formed by the producer's criteria of selection (a most unlikely prospect), those who do not get the product will be disappointed. They are unlikely to accept the producer's criteria as reasonable. And this will hold regardless of what these criteria might be. The very necessity of rationing which forces the producer to select also insures that he will have to make those left out rather unhappy.

We should not exaggerate the difference between this case and the market. Rationing takes place in every market. Rationing in ordinary markets, however, for automobiles as for other things, is accomplished via the price mechanism.

The ability to pay the market price becomes the objective criterion that distinguishes buyers from nonbuyers. And those hopeful consumers who cannot afford the market price for an article must feel, in one sense, similar to those left out under any rationing scheme. But there remains a major difference. The objectivity or impersonal character of the price mechanism reduces the arbitrary discriminatory power of the producer. The disappointment is not personalized. In order to be successful, the demander has only to meet the current price. There is no need for any fawning before the producer to secure subjectively determined favors.

## Selection of Quantity to Be Supplied

In this discussion, here and elsewhere, we recognize no supermen. The producers, whether of automobiles or of education, are ordinary mortals. They are little different from you and me. They are neither more nor less self-seeking. They are forced by institutional circumstances to make subjective or personal choices among potential consumers. And they are, in fact, doing "what comes naturally" to them when they behave so as to enhance their own comforts. Indeed, they would be behaving perversely if these should be neglected. They, therefore, appoint as consumers those who best fit their own subjectively determined criteria, whatever these might be.

Given the inexhaustible number of potential consumers, however, should we be surprised when producers also

restrict output—which, at best, may be vaguely defined—
below maximum limits? Producers will not only decide
whom from among their many potential consumers to
favor; they will also decide *how many* of these to favor
with their blessings. How, then, will they choose the rate
of delivery, the rate of output? They must once again select
that rate which best accords with their own priorities.
Their own criteria for "orderly" operation must once again
prevail. It would seem evident that the aesthetically satisfying rate will be considerably lower than that rate which
would fully exhaust producer capabilities.

## Selection of Quality of Product

We have isolated two dimensions of the producer's behavior. His selection of some preferred set from among all
potential demanders is one. His selection of some preferred
output is the other. What can we say about producer behavior along a third dimension, the quality of the product offered?

Here lies perhaps the most bizarre feature of the whole
institutional structure. Quality variables or components
will always be adjusted so as to meet the utility of the producer rather than that of the consumer or user. There is no
clear feedback which expresses consumer preferences in
this instance. The large number of potential consumers insures that all of the product supplied will be taken. The
producer, therefore, behaves quite normally when he uni-
laterally chooses the quality-mix that meets his own pre-

ferred standards. His consumers are like those Henry **Ford** once thought were his. They could choose any color of automobile—so long as it was black—provided that black happened to be the producer's own favorite and only color.

Since quality is a vector with many dimensional components, the use of general terms such as "high-quality" tends to be misleading. Nonetheless, by ordinary usage, producer preferences would probably dictate "high-quality" items, with little or no variety of quality dimensions. In our automobile example, we should predict that relatively long-lived and durable automobiles would be supplied. They would reflect a certain Veblenian "pride of workmanship," styles would be few in number, and these would change relatively slowly over time. But the desires, tastes, or preferences of consumers would not directly exert an influence on the relevant quality decisions. Once again, then, is it to be wondered that consumers could be observed to be frustrated, unhappy, and dissatisfied with the products they are offered?

## The Education-Producing "Faculty": The University

Of course, automobiles are not like educational services— especially services supplied by faculties in a university structure. Nevertheless, the three essential features of the peculiar institutional structure that we have imposed on our hypothetical automobile industry extend into any honest description of the behavior of university faculties. Faculties supply a product that is given away (or sold below cost) to consumers. Inevitably, there are many more applicants for university places than can be supplied. Faculties therefore, must establish criteria for selecting from among the many applicants. This is done by rationing the available places in accordance with some set of priorities. In setting these, faculties are naturally guided by their own utility functions, and do not behave much differently from ordinary men. They will tend to select applicants on some basis that insures faculty satisfaction.

Again, we are allowed to make some plausible predictions. Faculties generally prefer to work with "good" students. Those who have established good academic grade records or test scores in lower schools will effectively be preferred to those who have not accumulated such scores. Convenient means of sorting will be worked out and applied. And the process will continue as if it were uniquely based on "scientific" criteria. If, on the other hand, faculties disregard Julien Benda's warning, and begin to take seriously the modern nonsense about the university's current social purpose, they may set up entrance criteria which reflect objectives designed to "save the world." This may lead to admittance of those who might be least able to meet rigorous tests. In fact, what we observe around us in 1970 is some combination of these two extremes. High entrance requirements are applied, and rigorously so, to "normal" students, and entrance requirements are deliberately waived for "underprivileged" students—especially for those from ethnic minorities. The great middle group is excluded, with resulting dissatisfaction and a great potential for general public opposition.

The shift of admission criteria from rigid reliance on academic achievement painfully exposes the personal and nonobjective aspects of the present rationing process. Within limits, the academician could plausibly argue that criteria for university admission which were based on school records and test scores were "scientifically objective." Again within limits, he could cite a substantial accumulation of experience and wide agreement among "experts." What is more, such criteria have generally allowed the admissions officer, or faculty committee, charged with administering the system, to avoid the criticism of personal favoritism. The evolution of such rules and procedures within faculty-dominated institutions has insured, of course, that the results reflected faculty preferences for "good" students, as defined by these rules. For the specialized and probably temporary admissions officer these rules have existed as objective data.

In short, then, academic criteria for university admissions reflect the personal preferences and prejudices of faculties. This is a truth that should not and cannot be denied. How, therefore, can such criteria be held as sacrosanct? Still worse, changes and departures from these criteria, to allow the admission of "underprivileged" students, also reflect faculty preferences and prejudices. This, too, cannot be denied. But in shifting from almost exclusive reliance on one rationing scheme to the partial adoption of another, the myth of objectivity has been laid bare. Faculties now face accelerating criticism from disappointed applicants for precisely these reasons. Consider the potential student who is denied admission because he fails to meet a specific test score or because he fails to obtain the required decile ranking in his high school performance. Relatively complacent when he is refused a university place, he will naturally become aroused when he recognizes that other students, who do no better and perhaps worse on these same criteria, are awarded places.

## How Many Students Shall Be Admitted?

Faculty preferences are also reflected in determining the total number of university places that are to be supplied. Faculties and administrations secure relatively little direct benefit from expanding the number of places. They do secure indirect benefits because total output is measured in part by the number of graduates. There will be a trade-off between the quantity of students admitted and the usage of available staff and facilities, and the result will be a compromise of sorts.

If, in fact, faculties should be completely immune from feedbacks, either from taxpayers or from students, as some considerable part of faculty behavior seems to assume, we could make quite definite predictions about student numbers. In such a case, faculties would restrict numbers greatly to the point where their own satisfaction is maximized. They would admit only a number sufficient to provide the maximal faculty-student interaction—the ideal here being perhaps the Oxford tutorial structure. Small classes, seminar instruction, individual tutorials—these would characterize the university whose faculty is wholly immune from consumer or financier controls. But there would probably still be a relatively small number of students admitted. Universities generally would not go the way of All Souls.

When we look at the faculty control of student numbers, however, we cannot neglect the relevant constraints. Here faculty-administration freedom of action is limited by assessment of the effects of numbers on financial support by taxpayers or donors. A few starry-eyed faculty members (to whom finance is a grubby reminder of capitalist oppression) push for ideal arrangements such as tutorials, honors, personal supervision of good students, or personal assistance to a few underprivileged students. But even these visionaries recognize that universities could not be viable under dominance of their ideas. Most administrators and many faculty members acknowledge that production is measured in part by numbers. They necessarily make trade-offs between quantity and faculty satisfaction.

The institutional constraints do not, however, allow faculty-administrator rewards to vary closely with numbers of students graduated. Unlike the administrator, the faculty member rarely secures a higher salary directly as a result of a larger enrollment. He cannot convert student numbers into dollars which he can privately enjoy. The institutional structure forces him to secure benefits from large numbers indirectly through enlarged facilities. It will be useful to trace the procedure here.

## Faculties: Producers Who Do Not Sell

At all times and everywhere, existing staff claims to be overworked and existing facilities of universities are overcrowded. If you do not believe this, ask any staff member of any university. Of course, these are meaningless terms unless they are measured in relation to some standard. And the faculty member who tells you that he is "overworked" and his facilities "overcrowded" is honestly responding because he is measuring existing facilities against his own ideal standards. The latter embody few students and spacious, luxuriously furnished, fully equipped laboratories and research facilities. It should not be surprising that, relative to these standards, the faculty is overworked and space overcrowded. His complaints are continuous, and it is here that the indirect relationship between student numbers and financial support emerges. Faculties can rarely succeed in convincing taxpayers and other donors to increase financial support for them without increasing the number of students. Pointing to increased enrollments is a sure means of generating additional support. Realistically, the implication is that taxpayers establish standards in the basis of traditional staff-student and student-faculty ratios.

The likely result is that the ratio of student numbers to staff and facility sizes is larger than desired by faculties, but smaller than what would be observed if faculties should be able directly to convert financial support into salaries. As a simple conceptual experiment, ask yourself what any university faculty would do if offered the opportunity to increase staff-faculty salaries dollar-for-dollar with cost reductions in facilities, and proportionately with increases in student numbers. We should expect to see facilities more fully utilized, and faculties more fully occupied with instructional duties than at present. This can only be a conceptual experiment. Syndicalist pressure would prevent such experiments from happening in reality. The fate of Parsons College in Iowa at the hands of accrediting agencies is a case at hand.

## Quality of Service

There are many dimensions to the service of university education. We are neither especially qualified nor especially interested in discussion of the attributes of "good" education—or, as in this case, a "good" university curriculum and instructional procedure and organization. Perhaps the most striking economic characteristic of educational quality is independent of its specifics. This is that quality chosen almost exclusively by those who supply the service (university faculties) rather than by those who consume (university students). As suggested in Chapter 1, the peculiarity of education as a product or service makes consumer preference less relevant here than in the case of ordinary goods and services, such as appendectomies, apples, or automobiles. Nevertheless, the absence of ultimate student-consumer control over the quality-mix has effects that can be examined regardless of what may be preferred as the service device. The fact that producers select the quality of what they supply with little, or no direct, feedbacks from consumers yields predictable consequences.

46

## Faculties: Producers Who Do Not Sell

The educational mix that is offered will represent faculty preferences. In itself, this is an empty statement. But it ceases to be so when we say something about what these preferences are. Curriculum, university organization, instructional procedure—they will all remain almost immune from variations in student-consumers' tastes. We should, therefore, predict reasonable stability in these offerings over time. Innovation will not be a characteristic of faculty-controlled quality. Quality standards, defined in terms of customary ways of doing traditional things, will develop and persevere. So long as existing subject matter and methods please the "Establishment," there will emerge relatively few pressures for change. For the most part, faculties will continue to teach what they themselves were taught. It is *costly* to offer new subject matter. And, what amounts to more, for the faculty member there are few *offsetting* benefits. Lecture notes once finished require only the occasional updating. And even then this holds only in some disciplines. Once established, particular program offerings will prove almost impossible to discontinue, regardless of the state of student demands. New programs and methods will be resisted. This will be primarily because they offer little reward rather than on the basis of plausible argument in defense of established procedures.

This amounts to supporting the claim that faculties are conservative. The simple analysis shows us, however, that the conservatism of faculties has no ideological or philosophical base. It is a kind of conservatism that stems almost exclusively from the structure of the university itself.

## Academic Tenure

The procedures for selecting, retaining, and promoting faculty personnel represent an important part of the quality of the services that a university provides. One aspect of these procedures, academic tenure, is important enough to warrant separate discussion. In academic tenure, we find one of the root causes of the chaos that we observe.

As we have already noted, faculties are like ordinary men. If and when offered the opportunity, men will choose arrangements that provide them with the widest range of choices. No man will deliberately close off his options when, with little cost, he can keep them open. Tenure is merely one specific instance of this universal behavioral trait.

Ideally, any employee, in any position, be it large or small, prefers to have the option of remaining in that position, and of leaving it when better alternatives appear elsewhere. Job security is important to any man. But on the other side, any employer prefers to have the option of dismissing an employee when and if he desires to do so. Job security is seldom an asset to an employer. It normally involves a cost of doing business. This is why in the commercial world we expect employees and employers to negotiate arrangements concerning job security.

In the strange world of academia, however, no such negotiation goes on except for temporary appointments offered to junior staff members. Since faculties determine procedures and methods of university operation, almost without outside control, it is readily predictable that job-security arrangements will generally characterize personnel policy. This prediction is amply confirmed by the importance attached to academic tenure in universities. Faculties ardently defend tenure as a necessary part of academic freedom.

Ideally considered, tenure isolates the professional scholar from the pressures that the economic nexus imposes on ordinary men. Freed from such pressures, the scholar follows truth where it may lead, regardless of the consequences. Beyond this, the tenure-protected scholar "courageously" speaks out on, and supports, currently unpopular causes, exemplifying integrity of conscience in *vox populi* hysteria. It is one thing to defend academic tenure as a means of insuring that the scholar can pursue truth steadfastly without economic temptation. But it is quite another thing to extend such defense to protect the "intellectual" who desires to propagandize his own personal or party values in an university-college environment. Economically considered, tenure breaks the economic nexus, and in so doing, it reduces the potential penalties that external forces can impose on the scholar. But tenure also reduces the costs borne by the pseudo-scholar when he personally violates the principle of academic freedom, behaviorally interpreted, by departing from his traditional role as a detached truth-seeker. There is simply no legitimate defense of tenure for the academician who conceives his role to be the *politicization* of the university.

We need not elaborate this argument here. Economic analysis suggests merely that faculties, composed as they are of both genuine and false scholars, can be expected to defend tenure as an institution. Could they be expected to do otherwise? To them, as faculties, tenure costs little. And the maintenance of rights in university employment surely provides benefits. In fact, if faculties did *not* regard tenure as being important they would be perverse indeed. On the other hand, the outside observer, looking on university organization, should recognize tenure for what it is. It is basically a means for making life easy for the faculty member with both the good and the bad consequences suggested. And, as we expect to discuss in a later chapter, the one-sidedness of tenure provides a major cause for the university chaos that we currently witness. Secure in their university positions, faculty members (and this includes most members of university administrations) have no genuine incentive for standing up to internal revolutionary pressures. Ordinary men become courageous only when something they value highly is threatened. Faculties are made up of quite ordinary men. Given the university structure, student unrest and terror can hardly pose direct threats to faculty employment, pension rights, and so forth. If they did, backbones would have stiffened with amazing rapidity throughout modern academia.

## The Scholar's Role and Routine

Closely related to academic tenure are certain other procedures and methods that characterize the position of the fac-
ulty-scholar. These, too, are aspects of educational quality.
But they are predictably aimed at making the position of
the scholar-teacher as pleasant as it may be possible. Financial remuneration is earned on an academic year or annual
basis. And faculty members do not punch time clocks. Nor
do they turn in reports of their own attendance. They are
given almost completely free rein to organize instruction as
they desire. As compared with research, governmental, or
industrial positions, the routine of the university scholar is a
highly esteemed one. It is, therefore, little wonder that faculty salaries fall below salaries for comparably trained personnel in nonuniversity positions. Much of the faculty
member's reward is made up of nontaxable, nonmonetary
perquisites of university life. Recalling Adam Smith's example of the "executioner," we can readily attribute the relevant differential to the relative agreeableness of the employment.

But this characteristic, too, has deleterious effects. Faculty members are not directly harmed when student demonstrations and strikes break out. There are no significant
traceable consequences which they themselves directly suffer. Indeed, in one sense, faculty members may even secure

benefits. If student rioters shut down a university, faculty members go on receiving payment for not teaching. Hence, within limits, there are short-run gains to faculties from university strikes. Again, as a conceptual experiment, think how the present turmoil might be affected if faculty members should be paid strictly on the basis of the number of student-class hours of instruction. In such a case, any termination or disruption of the educational process would cause faculty members to suffer direct personal financial losses. It is almost tantalizing to imagine the attitude of faculties toward student unrest that this simple change in compensation would generate. Just as a student-loan, full tuition scheme might lead the vast majority of otherwise apathetic students into developing the desired antirevolutionary mood, the relative impossibility of enjoying "unearned salaries" might similarly coax faculties into more sensible behavior than they are often inclined to display. (It may be instructively noted that perhaps the gravest flaw in modern democracies is the almost mandatory aloofness imposed on their citizens, especially regarding matters of social urgency. In contrast, the original Athenian model was squarely based on participation inspired by a direct property right in the status quo and the set of ideals it represented.)

## Faculty Democracy

Faculties are not monolithic units. They are groups of men, each of whom behaves in his own way. To this point we have not worried about the way "faculties" make decisions on university policy. We can no longer neglect this question.

University tradition embodies faculty "democracy," and faculties are supposed to control university policy. Though important decisions are supposed to be reached democratically, within a framework of faculty control, this whole tradition is honored more in the breach than in the observance. In many cases, administrators and not faculties determine university policy. Decisions are often made by authoritarian rather than by democratic methods. We want, however, to evaluate university procedures in their revered and traditional setting and not in some deviant, if descriptive, embodiment. What can we say about faculty democracy when this exists as a genuine article?

Democracies, of course, exist and they are loved as such. But why should *faculties* be democratic? Few seem to be worrying about this elementary question. Democracy is basically a means of reaching group decisions. It is a means through which individuals participate in the formation of decisions that must then be applied to all who are members of the participating group. This is the fundamental logic of democracy as a governmental process. And it was precisely this kind of logic that was presumed applicable to the isolated "community of scholars" in the Middle Ages—the forerunner of the modern university. Yet few have noticed that this logic does not extend to the making of decisions that have their major impact on *others* than members of the participating group. There seems to be no rational basis, in economics or in ethics, for suggesting that faculty democracy "should" control modern universities. Decisions made here are not at all akin to those made in the medieval community of scholars where all affected by decisions were participants in the process. Policy in modern universities directly affects students and taxpayers who are not members of the participating faculty group. It follows that decisions reached democratically by faculties can be equally or even more oppressive to the persons thereby affected than those reached by authoritarian administrators. Evidently, this adds further explanation for the chaos we see everywhere around us. In fact, authoritarian policy might be notably more sensitive to the demands of clientele than democratic faculty policy.

At this point, an important economic aspect of faculty democracy must be noted. All faculty members participate. But some participate more fully than others. This Orwellian variant has predictable consequences. Under full-fledged faculty democracy, how do the various persons actually influence final outcomes? With democracy in all its forms, decisions are costly to make, and faculty-wide referenda on all issues would be impractical if not absurd. Representative assemblies act for faculties, therefore, and even within such assemblies division and debate must be limited severely. The yeoman work must be done in committees. And faculty democracy like any other large democracy, properly translated, means governance through committees.

Who serves on faculty committees? Anyone who knows the modern university knows the answer. Faculty committees are staffed voluntarily by those who want to serve. Who should want to serve? This has an economic answer. Faculty members who volunteer for committees are those who place the lowest value on alternative uses of their time. Committee service is time-consuming—fantastically so—and a faculty member who volunteers for such work necessarily sacrifices other time-consuming objectives. He values these objectives more or less highly, depending on his own skills and talents. The productive research-worker or teacher, who devotes his time valuably to research, writing, and instructional preparation, will find committee service extremely costly. The faculty drone, by contrast, who does little or no research, no writing, and teaches pedestrian material with little critical preparation, will find committee work more rewarding than his colleagues. Our economics tells us, therefore, that in normal circumstances faculty committees will be staffed by the less imaginative members of the university community. There are, of course, exceptions to every generalization and this is itself no exception. But the tendency outlined seems evident.

If our hypothesis here is valid, if faculty control is dominated by the pedestrian members of academia, we might

ment to assume that students are admitted at zero tuition and that taxpayers exercise only nominal control over university policy and structure. We shall change our discussion only by assuming that more than one university exists. We want to consider the effects of competition both among universities and among schools and departments within universities.

It is at once evident that any lessening of a monopoly position reduces the discretionary range open to decision-makers. Competition will take place among universities, and schools, for students; and among universities for faculty members. Let us consider these two cases separately.

Let students who meet admissions standards be allowed to choose among several universities. If the latter offer their services at zero tuition, students will select the opportunity that seems most inviting. If universities are in broad and general agreement on admissions criteria, if they all want "good" students, there will have to be some pressure on faculties to make their programs attractive to students. Net attractiveness to students involves many components. But only some of these are under faculty control. Within limits, of course, facilities may be made more attractive, curriculum can be made more relevant to apparent student demands, instructional methods can be adjusted to allow more student freedom, and so forth. But if forced to compete along any of these lines, faculties find their own satisfactions reduced. Any shift toward making the university more attractive to students involves costs to faculties. To the extent that is possible, therefore, they will resist such shifts. And, if they recognize that interuniversity competition is the likely source, they will almost certainly seek out ways and means to reduce this competition to minimal proportions. Agreements among universities will emerge to limit sharply the degree of university differentiation of product. If various universities can agree broadly on the criteria for admissions, for numbers, and for product quality, any incentive for students to shop around is accordingly reduced. This is, of course, what we observe.

In addition, there will be more and more efforts exerted toward incorporating separately functioning units into a monolithic administrative system. California again provides a telling example. Its nine campuses are organized within the same university structure which, operated as a single unit, tends to insure minimization of intercampus differentiation. Berkeley and UCLA, the two major units in the system, offer substantially the same curriculum, the same methods, and the same procedures. Competition for students is effectively minimized by the exercise of control by university-wide committees. Furthermore, a formal proposal was made in early 1969 to amalgamate the massive nine-campus system with the even larger state college system, creating thereby the so-called super-university.

In the United States, competition among separate universities for faculty members is perhaps more effective than competition for students. In Europe, this is less true. If universities are faced with the necessity of competing among themselves for faculty members, they must, to an extent, organize their arrangements so as to make opportunities attractive for the more productive scholars and teachers. To this extent, the dominance of the mediocrities in faculty committee government is reduced. General university policy must reflect at least partially the preferences of the better scholars. These need not, of course, be any closer to the preferences of the students. Attempts are also made to stifle university competition for faculty personnel. Cartel agreements among universities reduce the "raiding" of faculty talent. Once again California provides an excellent example. Different units of the university cannot compete among themselves for faculty personnel on a financial basis. Nation-wide competition among the several state systems and between these and private units exists, however, and cartel agreements are not effective over large numbers. In European countries, on the other hand, interuniversity competition for faculty is less prevalent because higher education tends to be more directly controlled by central governments. Standardized salary scales are imposed on a national basis, and this has the effect of reducing interuniversity mobility of scholars. Some competition does exist but universities are forced to compete in nonfinancial attractiveness.

In sum, competition among universities for students and for scholars mitigates somewhat the starkness of the predictions made about university structure. But the essential features of this structure remain as they have been outlined. Faculties control universities more or less as free-floating islands, moored neither to the demands and desires of those who consume their product, the students, nor to the demands and desires of those who supply the resources, the taxpayers. University faculties are unique in their freedom to maximize their own utilities without normal economic constraints. "Academic freedom" has genuine economic content, and the intense faculty defense of this freedom is indeed predictable on grounds of very elementary economics. Whether or not this freedom is socially justifiable is another question, and it is one that we have no need to discuss in this book.

*Intentionally or not, with foresight or not, we keep the fees low in order to accommodate less wealthy, more needy but deserving students. Low fees enable us (the faculty) to select students according to a non-money criterion. I select the better learners and smarter people who obviously "deserve" a higher education. How easy to swallow that self-serving contention!*

*The same reasoning could be applied elsewhere. Concerts should be free and financed by the state, so that musicians can select the audience, admitting those who have the keenest ear and are best at making music themselves. Less discerning people can do other things. After all, there is no sense in wasting music on those less able to appreciate it. . . .*

*Or if we are couturiers and dress makers, we will let only the most beautiful women have the best clothes. The average woman can wear her shapeless, less expensive dress. How wasteful to spend hundreds of pounds on a woman of hopeless figure, while there are women who, if beautifully dressed, would provide external benefits to the rest of society. Clearly, on the external-benefit count alone, clothing should be distributed as is education. . . .*

*Couturiers have long advocated that the state finance dressmaking, with zero prices for clothing, so that they too can select their clients with the gracious social beneficial care that we teachers employ. But not until the designers get tax-supported endowment subsidy, or non-profit dress design and manufacturing institutions, will they be able to serve society as well as we teachers do.*

Armen A. Alchian, *Pricing and Society*
(London: The Institute of Economic
Affairs, 1967)

# Chapter 4

# *Taxpayers: Owners Who Do Not Control*

Modern universities are common property. They are in the domain of the commonwealth. They are not the self-sufficient, isolated monastic communities which, centuries past, provided the origins of many features of academic organization and administration. The modern university or college draws its sustenance from—and, in fact, depends for its very life upon—the whole community. This generalization holds whether we refer to the nationally supported university systems in Europe, to the characteristic state universities in the United States, or to the so-called private universities. The latter are now sufficiently dependent on public largesse that Clark Kerr has called them federal grant universities—and this apart from the indirect support secured through federal tax deductions. Without massive and continuing financial support from the community at large, the modern university as presently constituted would swiftly collapse.

This fact is not in question. What is rather surprising is the extent to which so simple and obvious a truth can be ignored in the behavior of those who are involved in financing, producing, and consuming university education. Neither students, nor faculties, nor citizens-as-taxpayers behave as if the universities are public dependencies. The university is treated, by all groups alike, as if it retains characteristics of the self-supporting monastic community of scholars. It is idolized as if it were serving God in its chosen way—and, therefore, answerable only to God. We exaggerate somewhat, of course, but the metaphor is appropriate. Modern universities have been able, although perhaps not deliberately, to sustain a gigantic myth about the necessary and inviolable independence of academia from those upon whom it depends for support.

In part the myth has been accepted because academic independence has "paid off"—and not only to the academicians. The release of science from the straitjacket of the church hierarchy facilitated much of the technological progress since 1543. But it is important to recognize that public or governmental investment in, and support of, university education has assumed massive proportions only during the years after World War II. In all of the Western world, we have experienced, quite literally, a quantum jump in the numbers of persons seeking and getting education at university level, both absolutely and proportionately. The academic independence that produced the scientific and technological revolution cannot reasonably be called upon to justify the academic license that is nowadays exercised by the sometime mediocrities who carry out instructional duties *en masse*— and who, as we have already indicated, effectively control the modern universities. It is one thing to protect the genuinely productive scholar or scientist from the interfering political demagogue who may seek short-run advantage. It is quite another to erect and preserve barriers to political control over the pseudo-scholar who uses his university platform to foment class, race, and national hatred. As they are organized at present, universities make no distinction between two groups on their staff. The dominant assumption has been that the dangers of political control over the former are more severe than the dangers of the absence of such control over the latter. As the embattled acting president of San Francisco State College, Dr. S. I. Hayakawa, noted in early 1969, academic responses in the late 1960's were conditioned by the fears of external political interference aroused by the McCarthyism of the early 1950's. As a result, appropriate avenues for responsible political controls of the internal threats and disruptions by students and faculty were effectively closed. Hayakawa provided an analogy with the 1941 defenses of Singapore. Perhaps the chaos that we see about us should make even self-seeking academicians wonder whether or not the precarious independence of existing university systems is necessarily an attribute of the "good" postrevolution academic society.

## The Divorce of Ownership and Control

For almost half a century, economists have been concerned about the divorce of ownership from control in the modern business corporation. Corporate management has been alleged to hold power to make decisions that are contrary to the interests of the stockholders—who are, of course, the legal owners of the corporations. Whether and to what extent management does act against the owners' interest remains a question. Is it not singular that few economists have applied the same analysis to their own institution, the university, where the separation of ownership from effective control is far more complete? Within the limits imposed by the costs of organizing proxy fights, corporate management does exercise a range of discretionary power within which its own interests may be furthered. Beyond these limits, however, management must give due regard to stockholders' wealth interests or face the threat of replacement either directly or through a takeover bid. No such limits are imposed on the management of the modern university—that is, the combined administrator-faculty hierarchy. No "market for university shares" exists which might allow outsiders or insiders to purchase rights entitling them to participate in management replacements or takeovers. In a genuine sense, modern university management does what it pleases. What is more, it pays little or no regard to the interests of the ultimate owners: the citizens of the community. Restrictions on mismanagement and inefficiency are notoriously indirect and remote. Citizens can exert an influence only through the extremely circuitous political process. Citizens in California, whom polls revealed to be seriously concerned about the chaos in the university and college systems in the late 1960's, had little recourse other than "filing" complaints with their political leaders. These leaders, in their turn, found it necessary to implement change through relatively inactive and cumbersome boards of regents or trustees. And, in the last analysis, these latter could only act through the power of appointment and dismissal of administrative officials.

As James Ridgeway has noted, America's 2,200 colleges and universities form the largest group of quasi-secret organizations in the country. They have been so successful in safeguarding their privacy, particularly with respect to their finances, that few are aware of the extent to which the world of higher education actually does resemble a conglomerate corporation. Not much imagination is needed to suggest what might follow should a market in university shares develop and universities formally turn into corporations. It is almost inconceivable that acute investors, on the lookout for inefficient corporations to take over, could find a more juicy plum to snatch away than the University of California—although the London School of Economics would provide an excellent counterpart in England.

## Why Do Taxpayers Pay?

As we have repeatedly emphasized, university-college education is expensive. Its support requires economic resources. Professors do not work for peanuts or for the pleasure of pedagogy. Laboratories, libraries, lawns—they all cost money. The predominant share of this cost (especially if we neglect the foregone earnings of students during their university years) is borne by the general taxpayer. His share varies somewhat from one university-college system to another, since it must be dependent on the specific level of tuition charges and fees in existence. Even in the "private" universities, where tuition charges are not low, the student (or his family) pays only a part of the total cost of providing the university education that he receives. The remainder is paid by the taxpayer—whether through research grant support or favorable tax treatment to donors—and by the private donors themselves. The latter exercise little more, and often much less, control than do the taxpayers. Our discussion will not be grossly unrepresentative, therefore, if we continue to devote our main attention to the tax-supported, tuition-free, university system.

If universities depend on taxpayer support, why do taxpayers, as represented by their political leaders, fail to exert more controls over the scarce resources that they in effect give up?

Sheer sizes of political groups no doubt provide part of the answer. A single person's share in the university-college system becomes very small when the constituency includes millions. There is simply no incentive, therefore, for the individual citizen to initiate private or voluntary group action aimed at controlling commonly owned institutional systems. Here we have the so-called free rider problem applied in reverse. In modern public-goods theory, the tendency of the individual to behave as a "free rider" is often adduced to explain why governmental or public financing is required for certain goods and services which must be commonly shared by all members of the political community. The reverse twist is applicable here. An equivalent tendency exists for the individual to acquiesce in the continued financing of whatever goods and services governments may have commenced to provide. The selfsame traits that inhibit individual and voluntary creation of a major university independently of governmental action are apparent here. Individual or voluntary criticism and subsequent control of a major university system are inhibited once such a system has been established as a going concern with governmental financing.

There is more to this phenomenon, however, and the second explanation appears to be a more powerful one. Just what do individual taxpayers think they are "buying" with their tax dollars? What are they getting with their funds? What benefit do they enjoy by releasing scarce budgetary resources, which could be used to provide alternative private or public goods and services? If tax dollars should be

68

withdrawn from university-college financing, taxpayers could have either more apples and automobiles or more parks and policemen. Why do so many voters vote for candidates and parties who promise to provide more and more budgetary outlays on higher education? Clearly, enough voters must think that their tax effort provides something in return.

We have already referred to the problems that arise when we try to define "the product" that university education embodies. Education is not like apples, automobiles, parks, or policemen. Higher education in particular is a time-consuming, resource-using experience through which young persons pass. What is more, they are expected to become "better" persons in the process—culturally, intellectually, economically, and otherwise. The rationale for governmental-taxpayer financing must, therefore, be based on some presumed social or community value attached to the experience. The clichés are familiar. Individuals are supposed to be "better" citizens with education than without it. Nevertheless, it is almost impossible to quantify or to objectify the characteristics of the educated person (which the community allegedly values), apart and different from those values that the person, himself, attaches to his university experience. As we have noted, economists have devoted a great deal of their attention in recent years to a capital investment approach to university-college training. To the extent that income-earning capacities are increased by education, as they seem to be, the value of the investment is directly available to the consumer. Increased incomes are earned by the man whose capacities are so changed as to be able to earn them, and not by others in the community. The capital investment approach provides, therefore, small basis upon which to argue in defense of massive governmental financial support. At best, this approach lends strength to policy efforts aimed at setting up guaranteed student-loan schemes to offset repayment risks.

If massive taxpayer support over and beyond this is to be explained, something else must be added. And whether or not we personally agree or associate ourselves with it, some such explanation must exist. The fact of the matter is that massive taxpayer support for university-college education is a reality. What are the external benefits to society at large which a majority of taxpayers seem to think is conferred by general university-college education? We can hardly explain the widespread political popularity of university financing by the simple self-interest of members of political coalitions catering to the families of college-age persons.

Further research and inquiry, critically conducted, may succeed in quantifying and identifying more precisely some of the external benefits that are sensed and valued by taxpayers. But here we want to suggest quite a different approach. Is it not possible that the general public values university education precisely because it cannot quantify the benefits? Is the positive value placed on university financing by taxpayers due largely to a certain mystique that surrounds "education," a mystique that causes individuals to look on education as an end in itself?

## Education and Charity

For confirmation, we need only to look at the income tax laws. Taxpayers are allowed deductions for contributions made to educational and to charitable institutions. Clearly, the implication is that the financing of education is akin to charitable giving. This is not, of course, a modern conception. Educational support and charity have been closely related for centuries.

But this plays havoc with the simple economics of goods and services. If individuals value higher education, not for the "product" that it generates, but instead for itself, as indeed seems to be the case, what more can be said? For our purposes, the more that can be said the better since it explains much of the reluctance of taxpayers, through their political representatives, to impose ordinary controls over the expenditure of funds in universities and colleges.

When we say that individuals value education for itself, and not for the results that it produces, we are saying that the valuation is placed on the input—on the outlay and investment made, rather than on the output or product that emerges from the process. Individuals may approve public financing of higher education because this financing, or tax sacrifice, is in itself a *moral act*. It is the performance of this *duty* which yields value directly to the actor. In other words, support of educational institutions through govern-

71

mental auspices may be, for the taxpayer-citizen, an expression of a Kantian good will. He approves because the act itself is good and not necessarily because it is predicted to yield consequences that see themselves to be desirable.

There is little doubt that much of the support for educational outlay stems from just such motives. Education is like charity, as perceived by the one who gives privately or publicly to his university, to his community fund, or to a program of poverty relief. But how does this help us to explain current university chaos? The logical chain here is more direct than almost anywhere else in our whole analysis of the institutional structure of the university. When that which is valued is the *act of giving*, the giver, whether he be private donor or public taxpayer, has little interest in the ultimate end product that his gift generates. Gordon Tullock has applied this conception imaginatively to explain why charities tend to be more inefficient operations than profit-seeking enterprises. But the explanation applies equally to universities, whether public or private. To the extent that owners or donors value the act of financing education, as opposed to valuing that which is financed, their own interests are effectively discharged once the act of financing is completed. There is then little or no gain to such an owner or donor from carefully imposed controls over agency operations. To such a person, the differences between "efficient" and "inefficient" operations become negligible. This would remain true even if agreement should be reached on how efficiency might be measured.

Evidence that this attitude is characteristic of many persons is not hard to locate. Different states compare educational achievements, not in terms of quantity or quality of product, but in terms of dollars spent. Surefire arguments for securing legislative support for expanded university financing are comparisons with other systems on the basis of dollars spent, not product generated. Think how a political candidate might fare by saying that he proposes a reduction in educational outlay while guaranteeing a larger effective output. For education all up and down the line, from lower schools to higher, *inputs are outputs* as these are evaluated by the taxpayer.

Under this explanatory rubric, the taxpayers-citizens, as owners of state university and college systems, are not irrational in their failure to impose controls over the uses of funds comparable to those imposed over more mundane or specifically definable products such as, say, highways. Once their investment is made, like a gift to the church, their duty has been fulfilled. Does not this, in itself, go a certain part of the way toward explaining the peculiar vulnerability of university structure to the modern revolutionary thrust?

## The Church, the State, and the University

Institutions can always be explained in part by their historical origins, and we have several times referred to the medieval sources of university structure. One important feature of modern academic organization and modern attitudes toward higher educational institutions can be traced to the intense struggle between church and state. The universities were arms of church power, and hence they were held to be outside the realm of state or governmental powers. This meant that the universities were subject to the canon law and not to the law of the state.

This heritage extends into the modern era when the financing of universities has been assumed by the state. Despite the shift in the economic support of higher education, the tradition of independence from political control has been vigorously maintained. Implicit in the attitudes toward universities has been the view that these institutions were to be answerable only to their own laws, internally derived and internally enforced. In fact, it can be said without exaggeration that the university has become, in the modern world, the nearest equivalent to the church of the Middle Ages. Its precincts are sacrosanct, and the suffering taxpayer is placed in a position not unlike that of the poor man who sacrificed bread in support of the magnificence of the church establishment in centuries past. This revered independence of the university from political control has reached absurd limits in some of the recent turmoil. The stridency with which the revolting students object to the simple exercise of the police power of the state on *state* university campuses, and the support that this secures from the community at large, attests to the continuing strength of the myth concerning the "rights" of academia to act in accordance with its own "moral" law.

74

# University Governing Boards

Systems of higher education include institutions that were deliberately designed to prevent taxpayers-citizens, through their elected political representatives, from controlling the operations of the universities and colleges. To avoid subjecting the educational institutions to the controls either of political leaders or of financing angels, governing boards were established to act as buffers between these and the academicians. All external influence, which means all effective public influence, over the universities is channelled through these governing boards—of trustees, regents, governors, visitors, and so forth—which nominally own the university-college facilities.

The organizational and functional details of such boards vary widely from one system to the other, as do the effective powers that they exercise. Description is not our purpose here but a few characteristics are worth noting because they seem almost universal. Governing boards tend to be composed of laymen who have established a degree of prominence in business or the professions, and who have demonstrated some interest in higher education, normally in the particular institution governed (usually as an alumni leader). Members are normally appointed by political leaders in the case of state universities, and their terms of service usually extend over several years. Board members hold full-time positions in their own professional and business capacities. Their functions as university-college governors are, therefore, not supposed to be and could not be time-consuming. In the United States, the standard pattern is one half-day per month during the academic year or eight full days per year. The boards do not, as a rule, have their own staffs, and members are rarely expected to do more than to participate in the actual meetings. Almost literally, governing boards of modern universities are expected to "rubber-stamp" policy actions initiated by university administrators and faculties. As presently constituted, the boards could do little else. They exist for the purpose of providing a pretense that effective external control is exercised on the internal authorities of the universities and colleges. But it is well recognized that, for all practical purposes, these internal authorities do just about as they please. The constraints imposed by the formal controls of the governing boards are generally not sufficient to modify substantially the behavior of those who determine university policy: the members of the administrations and faculties.

How does this weak control by externally appointed governing boards affect the behavior of faculties and administrators when any effect at all is present? In that lost paradise of academic independence before the onset of modern student unrest, a long-standing quasi-equilibrium was somehow maintained. Rules, procedures, methods, curricula—these embodied the results of a slowly moving evolutionary process in which the mutations that did occur insured the furtherance of the attractiveness of academia for faculties. Few policy changes took place, and those which were proposed were rarely dramatic or campus shattering. The institutional apathy of governing boards insured the continuity of things more or less as they were and had been for decades. The institutionally determined conservatism of faculties, mentioned in Chapter 3, was effectively preserved and fostered by the inertia of the governing boards. As suggested above, governing boards were conceived to serve the primary function of warding off undue external control, not the imposing of political control over faculty behavior.

All of this was drastically modified in the light of the student unrest which began in the mid-1960's. The inaction and inertia of the governing boards tended to leave faculties without an anchor upon which to base policy measures that had previously never been thought necessary. But as faculties and university administrations have been forced to retreat under militant student pressures, dramatic and sweeping changes in effective university operation have taken place. This has exposed an awesome gap in university governance. Boards which should have come into their own as a source of external control and ultimate community strength have seemed powerless to act—no doubt because of decades of inaction.

The point here can perhaps be made by an analogy. Children can be left outside to play, often quite alone and without close parental or adult supervision. When disputes arise, however, the strength of parents must be available for quick entry into the picture. Parents must retain ulti-

mate authority when disputes threaten to become dangerous. Disaster is courted when interference is either put off
for too long, or is naive when it is forthcoming. A case at
hand was the willingness of the Court of Governors at the
London School of Economics to acknowledge as a "miti-
gating circumstance" the fact that the "children" left the
buildings in good condition following the violent and un-
lawful occupation in October, 1968.

At an earlier point we referred to universities as free-
floating islands, moored neither to the demands of consumers nor to the controls of owners. The free-floating island
remains idyllic until the foul winds blow. But then some
harbor, some fixity, is desperately needed. Governing boards
fail to provide this in present university crises situations.
These boards have tended to allow faculties to fend for
themselves in the hope that firmness in the face of revolutionary pressures would emerge from within. This is, of
course, one possible outcome. Faculties may yet display the
courage to counter the terror that threatens their existence.
But an understanding of faculty decision processes lends
small hope to this result. Faculties and administrations find
it especially difficult to take positive decisions that involve
dramatic policy changes. In consequence, they tend to respond to threats posed by student violence and terror rather
than to forestall such threats themselves. For example, it is
almost inconceivable that the University of California faculty, in 1969, would have adopted a policy stating that all
students arrested in campus demonstrations should be sum-
marily expelled. Yet it is quite conceivable that, should such

a policy have been imposed externally by the Board of Regents, acting on behalf of the state, a large majority of the university faculty would have approved.

As we have suggested, the medieval heritage of the university as a church institution which was isolated from political control has carried over into modern times. But it is precisely in the absence of some ultimate nongovernmental but external control structure that the modern university differs drastically from its precursors. For the latter, the absence of state control directly implied the ultimate imposition of church control. For the modern university, by contrast, faculties and administrators are expected to find their own way out of the turmoil, a task for which these groups seem singularly ill-equipped to perform. Recognizing this, can we not make a plausible prediction? Does it not seem likely that the most effective responses to violence and terror will be found in those universities where the political power of the state is used with responsibility and in those nonstate universities where the controls remain vested in an effective church hierarchy? Does this not then suggest that the institutions most vulnerable to threats of terror are those where the ultimate external controls of either political or private agencies are most remote?

So far our analysis has been sufficiently general to be applicable to both private and public universities and to all the mixtures of these (two) that are found in established institutions. It is nonetheless essential that we note certain features of the analysis that are peculiarly relevant to specific institutional types. The particular vulnerability of the endowments of private universities and colleges must be mentioned here. These endowments represent wealth that is available for tapping. And, in many cases, it may well prove much easier to tap the existing endowment wealth of private universities than it is to tap the potential wealth of public universities represented in the tax base of the community. In the latter case, the ultimate and final response to terror and the threat of violence may be the refusal of the taxpayer, through his elected representatives, to provide further sources of finance for higher education. With the private university, which has a large endowment, no such ultimate institutional protection exists. Events at the Claremont Colleges in February, 1969 provide a striking corroboration of this hypothesis. Under the sheer threat of terror, which involved arson and the maiming of a college secretary by a bomb explosion, the faculty-administration decision-makers approved a plan to divert substantial funds from the endowment to satisfy militant student demands. Before Cornell's infamous capitulation, there was perhaps no more clearcut case of response to terror by submission. Had these Claremont Colleges been public institutions, without significant endowments, the faculties would have found it impossible to respond financially to the militant demands. At best, public institutions can change budgetary allocations within existing appropriations and can modify existing rules. They have no sitting ducks in the form of endowments with which to pay the ransom.

# Are Universities Owned at All?

This chapter's title refers to taxpayers-citizens as "owners" of universities and colleges. In a certain technical and legalistic sense, this is descriptively accurate. At the entrance to the University of California, there is a plaque which states that the physical facilities are the property of the regents of the university, acting as agents for the whole people of the state. With respect to physical assets, universities must be owned. And in the case of publicly supported systems, the location of ultimate property rights must be in the citizens of the taxing community, or their agents.

In a different conception, however, we may question whether or not the rights of ownership to a university are vested with any person or group. What does the right of ownership imply? Applied to a person, ownership implies rights to do certain things, to behave in some ways and not in others. This is true even in the simplest forms of ownership, such as landed property. The person who holds title to a piece of land is entitled to exclude others from this land for some purposes but not necessarily for all purposes. (For example, utility companies may be granted easements.) He is entitled to use the land in certain ways but not necessarily in all ways. For instance, he may not be able to modify the drainage system so as to flood his neighbor. Even with the simplest forms of ownership, therefore, there are varying restrictions on the specific rights that title to assets guarantees. Ownership is not a conception that can be defined in an abstract yet operational manner.

Once we depart from the simple patterns of ownership, such as land and physical assets, the structure of property rights becomes exceedingly complex. Who really owns that which is used in common by many persons? Who owns the city streets, the sidewalks? Each person, as potential user, has a right of access, but no person has the right to exclude others from access and usage. Viewed positively, each user has a property right. Each user is an owner. Viewed negatively, in terms of exclusion rights, no single person owns the street. Ownership in this sense usually is vested in the body politic, the community as a collectivity, which can, if and when it chooses, exclude some persons and not others.

The modern university is much more complex than either land or streets. If one looks at the university in terms of ownership, it immediately seems a very complex and interlinked chain of rights, duties, and obligations claimed and exercised by several well-defined groups in a peculiar sort of hierarchy. As we have already noted, many of the origins of the university stem from the Middle Ages, and this extends also to organization. The university can perhaps best be analyzed as a hangover of the feudal system. Viewed in terms of rights to carry on activities, students, faculties, administrators, and governing boards all share in ownership. These rights are presumably understood by all parties. This allocation and understanding of rights is based on long-established tradition and custom. Things are done by various parties and groups because this is the way things have been done—and this is reason enough. Indeed, one of the sources of current unrest is precisely the breakdown in the consensus on the rights and obligations that the university embodies. Viewed, therefore, in terms of rights of exclusion, the ownership structure of universities remains somewhat clouded. Since students cannot presumably exclude anyone, their rights of genuine ownership disappear in this negative conception. Faculties, in contrast, clearly have ownership rights, even in the sense of exclusion. They can exclude students, either from admission to the university, or from particular facilities.

It is just at this point, however, that the property rights in the university become hazy and ill-defined. Faculty-administrative rules can limit student entry into the community. These can also prevent student attendance at classes unless proper registration forms are filled out, or prevent student usage of library facilities under such conditions, and so forth. But can faculty rules prohibit student usage of the university's common grounds, its lawns, its quadrangles, its common rooms? Recall that it was precisely this sort of issue that, at least nominally, touched off the Berkeley demonstrations in 1964, one of the first outbreaks of student violence. Even more significantly perhaps, the basic issue in the "people's park" struggle at Berkeley in May, 1969 was the university's authority to determine the usage of land under its clear nominal ownership. The invasions of university buildings have become commonplace. Students claim what amounts to property rights in these common university facilities, and faculties have not been forceful in exerting their rights of exclusion. Governing boards, acting for the body politic, clearly do possess such rights in the strictest sense. They can exclude anyone from using university facilities, and this extends to students and faculties. These rights of ownership have atrophied from persistent delegation and lack of application, however, so much so that they can scarcely be called an effective set of rights. The ultimate right of the state, through its agents, to exclude students and faculties from university-college facilities, is what the militants fear most, and appropriately so. This is surely the source of their unceasing propaganda against "police on the campus." Militants have little or no fear of university faculties or university administrations. But they do fear the behavior of the external political community.

Faculties are reluctant to exclude students from university common grounds. This reluctance extends, perhaps surprisingly, beyond the common, to areas of universities that should, nominally at least, be strictly under faculty-administration control. How can we explain the reluctance of faculties and administrators to defend their apparent property rights here with vigor?

## The Marketability of Property

One explanation says simply that faculty members and university officials are spineless creatures, lacking in the simple courage that their forebears would have exhibited. But this is hardly an explanation at all. The question remains. Why do these men behave as they do in regard to students' invasion of what has been, by long-standing tradition and practice, strictly "private" property?

Only economic theory can supply the answer here. The individual members of the university community, whether these be nonfaculty staff, faculty personnel, administrative officials, or external governors, are placed in the role of holders of rights that they cannot convert into personal market values. This simple difference between common ownership and genuinely divisible private ownership has extremely important effects on personal behavior, as we have known since Aristotle. The behavioral difference can best be illustrated introspectively. Ask yourself whether or not you would defend your office in a university from invasion with the same strength and conviction that you would defend your office in your home? If the answer seems obvious, then ask yourself why you would behave so differently in the two instances. The student who invades and occupies the professor's university office imposes costs on the latter—costs in terms of time, inconvenience, and bother. But beyond these costs, even should his office be destroyed, the professor has lost nothing which carries for him a personally possessed marketable value—provided, of course, that his personal books and papers are not affected. Contrast this with an imagined student invasion and occupation of the professor's office in his home. Here something that does carry a personal marketable value is threatened. The incidence of destruction is both concentrated and explicit. And, once again, think how much differently faculty members might act in a university setting if they should be required to rent, lease, or purchase office facilities from the universities.

*The hedge-sparrow fed the cuckoo so long,*
*That it had it head bit off by it young.*
Shakespeare, *King Lear,*
Act I, iv.

# PART TWO

# Preface to Part Two

*We are not intellectual nihilists whose aim is to attack the university from another quarter. We have both been nurtured by and have enjoyed the liberties of the academic heritage. We think that we can recognize, as well as the next man, the value that this has represented in the advances of Western culture and civilization.*

*Our central purpose is to offer a limited and admittedly partial explanation of the university chaos that now threatens to destroy this heritage. In order to understand why the university seems to be particularly vulnerable to current revolutionary pressures, critical examination of the whole structure is required. As economists, we assess the university from an economic point of view. We provide an economic diagnosis. As it turns out, this makes our analysis appear as an exposé. We emphasize, however, that the straightforward application of one set of tools, those of elementary economic theory, in no way precludes our own personal appreciation of the special characteristics of higher education.*

*We should perhaps note that our analysis of university structure is not time-constrained. Precisely the same analysis could have been made by economists before the turmoil of the 1960's. But in the relative tranquility of the 1950's, an economic explanation of the practices and procedures of academic communities might have served little purpose. We rarely diagnose patients who exhibit few symptoms of illness. For in that bygone era, universities, as they were organized and as they performed, seemed to embody a reasonable balance of aims and objectives. But, alas, that world of the 1950's is no longer with us. Symptoms of illness are pervasive and university structure and traditions must now be re-evaluated. In fact, it is precisely because we place a high and positive value on the academic heritage that we have been moved to write this book at all. We see that which is valuable in academia on the way to being destroyed, often by arguments that are allegedly advanced in its own defense.*

*The house of straw that is the modern university has been laid bare in Part One. In Part Two, we begin with a paraeconomic sketch of the early responses to the revolutionary pressures. We then make some attempt to develop the new economics of violence. There follows a critical examination of the strategies of terror and the response to it. In a concluding chapter, we advance a few specific predictions and prophecies, some of which give grounds for cautious optimism. We suggest no nostrums, and we shall try to resist the ever-present temptation to indulge in precipitate prescription.*

# Chapter 5

# *The Coming of Confrontation*

University policy and structure, like other human institutions, will probably never reach utopian bliss. Bliss is inherently otherworldly—at least since man's rowdy exit from the Garden of Eden. We live, as we have always lived, in a world of change. For better or worse, history has also taught us that backwardness is the alternative to progress. When societies have not transformed themselves into launching pads capable of opening up new avenues to mankind, a process of decline has invariably set in.

New ideas in the world of politics and economics, massive developments in the physical sciences and (on a small scale) the social sciences, fresh tastes or patterns of expression and communication, novel styles of living, and modern ways of seeking happiness: all these, and endless other things, have made our society into something it was not. Whether seen in the context of years or decades, human society has been remarkable in mobilizing the emotions, the energy, and the idealism of generations, in preserving its survival in change. This is an undeniable truth. Yet one notable exception comes to mind: the university. In some respects, as Jencks and Riesman have noted, universities and colleges seem to have been designed for the very purpose of maintaining old standards. Rejecting change over many generations, universities today seem to find themselves on the threshold of collapse.

Can one reasonably speak of any dramatic differences between contemporary universities and those of decades past? Is it by accident only that we trace the origins of the universities to the Middle Ages and those of other social institutions to the Enlightenment or later? Universities have always made up a curious industry, but their structural stagnation seems more apparent in dynamic change, and especially so during a period when a quantum increase in the demands for higher education is taking place.

Is it so surprising that universities today should at last be reaping the fruits of their agelong "independence" from that creative evolutionary force which has swept through all those institutions of society that were more responsive to economic pressures? Was not the creeping foolishness of a tradition-bound system almost certain to explode one day into the contemporary nonsense?

How could the nature of goods and services in education

—just as, for that matter, quality anywhere else in the production process of an economy—have improved by consistently ignoring the preferences of those who are its purported beneficiaries, whether these be students or taxpayers? Besides, how often do revealed and presumed preferences in life coincide? The answers to all of these questions are plain and simple. The reasons behind the university revolution which most of us now have to suffer around us are beginning to emerge with clarity.

We are now witnessing a new phenomenon. Universities, which remained almost maximally insensitive in their response to student-customer preferences for generations, now seem to be developing the perversely opposite behavioral characteristic. Suddenly, they have become much more sensitive to student-consumer demands. Decision-makers in many of our leading institutions are, in fact, converging toward the realm of the hypersensitive—but with a difference. This newly acquired sensitivity seems to be almost exclusively responsive to excitational stimuli flowing from the violence and terror generated by a small set of highly unrepresentative student minorities. In the process, the largely inarticulated preferences of the great majority of students become more and more neglected. Perhaps more significantly, the university decision-makers, in responding favorably to the ever-accelerating "demands" of the revolutionary terrorists, dramatically decrease the traditional support of the nonacademic community. Are the constitutional controls embodied in long-standing traditions and exercised remotely by governing boards and faculties now to be replaced by the informal and ad hoc controls imposed by the few addicted to violence and terror?

## Straining the Equilibrium of the Past

Our application of economics to the university scene has suggested that much of the turmoil can be related to the existing policy and structure of our universities. We have explained the lack of student participation and influence in university policy-making. If students felt they could communicate more effectively with university faculties, they might be expected to limit their confrontation tactics. And they might be led to formulate their demands so as to use legitimate constitutional channels. We have shown, however, that changes in this direction have been prevented by the swelling impersonality and bureaucratization which has characterized the rationing process. Universities faced with a rising excess demand for their goods and services sense little need to respond more effectively to the consumers of these services. The basic message of Part One was the linking of student unrest to prevailing structural features involving a relative lack of student influence in the university decision-making process; and a variety of faculty behavioral traits leading to a progressive deterioration in the quality of the educational offering—both as such and in its comparative inability to reflect student preferences. We have interpreted the increasing chaos in the university community as a direct consequence of the highly traditionalist, almost feudal, university system which has failed to adapt itself to the desires of a society caught in a process of continuous transformation.

## Sources of Increased Student Disaffection

It is not difficult to see why the inherently idealistic character of studenthood, incessantly bombarded by the stimuli of a changing society, has served as a powerful catalyst here. After all, is it not to be expected that students, as a social stratum, should always be singularly responsive to political trends, to opportunities for action, to changes in social moods? The student child-man is a comparatively frustrated being, marginal in principle, a creature in transition between a situation of family dependence (for almost all forms of existence) and one that allows him to take up his own personal role in life. Is it, therefore, surprising that as youthful minds are beginning to open out and delight in the broad variety of human knowledge and experience, that their relative immaturity should induce them to develop absolute commitments and convictions to causes and ideas? Student behavior is seldom tempered by the ethic of responsibility. Concern among students for the *consequences* of action (which might lead to the recognition that it is also necessary to compromise among conflicting values in order to achieve whatever good may be feasible in any given set of practical circumstances) is indeed rare. "Free, free LSE, take it from the bourgeoisie!" The sound is good, it seems "new," it apparently shakes up the world —and so corrupt a world deserves at least that much. Here, in a nutshell, we have the motivation of the average student activist at the London School of Economics—or, for that matter, anywhere else. And if we inquire what is meant by all this, what it is that the student really wants, what he wishes to build instead, what his program is —the answer is equally absolute. "No program. First we will make the revolution, and then we will find out what for. That which exists is the *thesis*. We provide the *antithesis*. That which will emerge, the *synthesis*, is bound to represent an advanced stage of development." The absurdity of the Hegelian dialectic is lost in its rhetoric.

At this point, our first-day economics must be integrated with some elementary behavioral analysis in order to understand why the university equilibrium that was propped up by tradition was so noticeably disturbed by the revolutionary waves of the past decade in particular. Students have always been students, and they have behaved as such. What requires explanation is why this behavior has erupted into a problem of widespread social significance in the 1960's.

A variety of evidence suggests that the tensions flowing from the relative aggressiveness of modern society seriously affect the emotional stability of many university students, even among the most able of them. These tensions naturally find many different outlets. A pronounced propensity remains, however, for students to reject the highly competitive social system which forces them into their acute anx-

two different and far-reaching consequences. First, it has meant that the absolute number of students has become much greater than it once was, and that a relatively small percentage of the total student body, whether on a given campus or nationally, can look like a major force in absolute numbers. There are close to 200,000 students in Paris, so that 10 per cent of them were the 20,000 who took part in the Paris demonstrations. There are over 400,000 students in Tokyo, so that a small proportion of them can make twice as spectacular a demonstration—and so on and so forth, in the United States and elsewhere. Perhaps more important, however, this growth means that even without a relative increase in the proportion of students committed to disruptive tactics the possibilities of waging impressive subversive protests have dramatically increased. Second, as we have already explained in Part One, the increase in numbers of students has almost everywhere led to a deterioration of their position in terms of the educational offering they receive. Many countries have expanded the numbers of students, particularly in the humanities and social sciences, without increasing the size of the faculty and adequately expanding other relevant facilities. An increasing proportion of students has become subject to a much greater degree of impersonality, to less attention from faculty, and to more "repressive" university-wide congestion. Their generalized sense of insecurity—which inherently flows from their marginal position between family-parental dependence and personal independence—is consequently much greater than ever before. Students have increasingly lacked a clearcut

sense of their personal future. And this has become especially true since attending university ceased to be an elite activity. In sum, there is a greater objective basis today for student discontent and, at the same time, it has become easier
to mount effectively larger demonstrations. As one would
also expect, increasing pressures for university reform rein-
force the sources of concern for social reform, and vice
versa.

### External Events

The cozy equilibrium of the past, largely upheld by the
relatively *passive* behavior of the early postwar generation,
has been increasingly strained by the more recent activist
student minorities. Some of the basic conditions which
dampened internal ideological controversy during the 1940's
and 1950's have changed.

Essentially, the politics of these two decades were dominated by the international struggle against totalitarian ex-
pansionism. First, we had the Axis powers, and then Sta-
linist communism. In both instances, the threats to Western democracy, together with its institutions, were real and
awe-inspiring. The majority of liberal intellectuals, who
might otherwise have become acutely critical of domestic
institutions and practices, thus found themselves defending
their own societies against the totalitarian menace. As Seymour Lipset has also suggested, this period was effectively
broken by changes within the communist world, coupled
by an increasing awareness of the social conditions existing

in the (third) underdeveloped world. But, as ideological anticommunism lost a considerable part of its momentum, the absolutist character of younger intellectuals and students began to express itself in domestically directed political, social, and economic criticism. This change in the ideological climate, intensified by the discovery that the transformation of protest from mere words to the confrontation tactics of civil disobedience could be splendidly successful in a "spineless" environment, has contributed greatly to our present condition. The equilibrium of the whole tradition-bound university structure thus seems to be precariously in the balance, in the face of the rise of violence to universal prominence—and possibly esteem.

## Perverse Reaction Patterns

Another interesting phenomenon is evident. As administrative or faculty power decreases—as it becomes more and more severely limited with the spreading influence of the violent few—the greater the incentive for further student disruption and violence. The greater the violence, the greater the propensity of the university authorities to capitulate. The direction and ultimate conclusion of this reaction-spiral is obvious. A simple economic analogy would be a price or rationing mechanism which operated in such a fashion as to react to rising excess demand by *downward* adjustments in prices. There is no need for even elementary economics to label such a reaction process as perverse. Instead of generating a return toward some sort of stable equilibrium, the price reactions would, in and of themselves, make the pressure of excess demand more and more acute.

The observed weakening of faculty controls (faculty capitulation, in other words) in the face of threatened or actual violence is precisely the opposite pattern of response to that which a properly working, logically coherent, or self-adjusting mechanism of "punishments and rewards" would require. If any return toward stability is to be expected, faculty-administrative authority must be extended as violence increases. Persistent capitulation in the face of violence must tend to ultimate annihilation of the whole structure.

Of course, it may be argued that "feeding" violence with lower, as opposed to higher, degrees of "intransigence" would be the appropriate response over some relevant behavioral range—if the terrorists, themselves, exhibit perverse reaction patterns. In such a case, we might have to conclude that violence is best contained with less, not more, opposition. One could even add here that particularly in the case of group (as compared to individual) behavior such "lenience" would make more sense. It has even been said that the existence of punitive sanctions against extremist activism is pointless because those engaging in it have zero opportunity costs—and, therefore, nothing to lose. In short, the policy implication would be that student terrorists might cease to pound on the doors of the Establishment, as it were, if they were suddenly to find them wide open. Maybe. On the other hand, as Tom Hayden, one of the

New Left leaders, seems prone to stress in front of television cameras, everything in sight must first be destroyed in order to find out, second, what for. As in the other parts of our analysis, however, we prefer to assume that terrorists act "normally." This leads to the simple conclusion, as we see in the next chapters, that terror will increase if its rewards are increased or its costs are reduced. To base university (or social policy) on a denial of this simple principle seems manifest idiocy.

Several other explanations for the extraordinary indifference or tolerance of university authorities in the face of student violence also seem fully plausible. It will be particularly useful to ask how the initial deviations from constitutional behavior in the universities were tolerated in their *embryonic* stage. Why did student anarchy in its beginnings fail to attract the requisite rebukes? Why, instead, was it allowed to swell until it ultimately assumed its current proportions? How did it succeed in inflating to such dimensions as to be virtually dictating an accelerated faculty-administration "withdrawal," despite the latter's constant assurances that the contrary is in effect happening? In brief, how can we explain this remarkable insensitivity of university authorities at a time when a more sensitive pattern of response would have almost certainly not paved the way for the productivity of contemporary student terrorism? Perhaps student terrorism will prove the *locus classicus* of the ultimate success awaiting all "creeping advance" strategies, a triumphant show of the inevitability of gradualness. Can it be, in fact, that only gradual change is effective change? But more of this in Chapter 7.

## Equilibrium Shattered

Whatever its sources, the youthful "reformism" so emphasized during the past decade has surely been the most dramatic and direct instrument which has led to the disturbance of the equilibrium which was, at best, a precarious one. In recent years an increasing premium has been placed on being youthful and on taking seriously the opinions of the young. Throughout the world, the tendency to idolize youth and to deprecate age has been on the rise. Today, to look youthful, to behave youthfully, to adopt first the dances and next the political and social views which are identified with youth, has become the "in" thing to do. How surprising is it, therefore, that many adults in general, and certainly administrations and faculties of universities in particular, have consistently become more and more reluctant—even when they feel the need to disagree—to call students or youth sharply to task? Only a casual glance around us will immediately confirm that rather than emphasizing the worth of experience, long-term learning processes, hard work, and responsible or rational behavior, students have been encouraged to take independent new positions—which in turn become the latest and smartest pinnacles in socio-political fashion.

The young are no longer being trained in the ways of conduct known to be "decent" by their elders. The modern liberal generation has by now steeped itself in knowledge that the young are morally superior, more idealistic, and better motivated—whatever their crudity or vulgarity. Somehow, rights to absolute personal freedom that few others possess seem to have been institutionally issued to the few—particularly the revolting few—among the young. Society seems to be doing its best, thanks to its liberal academic reformers, to convince the nonactivists that only one set of *rights* are relevant, that all issues have only one "right" side, even if securing this involves burning down the city. In fact, this is a doctrine which, since the foundation of the First International in 1864, may yet prove that history does not necessarily ostracize to permanent oblivion movements which fail to take their chances the first-time around.

Violence and terror are ravaging the products of centuries of Western intellectual and aesthetic excellence. And our universities seem to be caught up in tragic acquiescence to the attitude that those who feel "sufficiently deep moral concern" about political (and, of course, nonacademic) issues have the right to protest, to demonstrate, to riot and even to assault the freedoms of others either within or without the university walls. This now pervasive attitude which allows anarchist departures from constitutional procedures so long as the "cause is good" was the hallmark of political leadership in the early 1960's. We have thus reached a state where a handful of improbable students on almost every campus in the world have succeeded in inflicting their ways upon everybody else. This has been achieved through a masterfully calculated, absolute contempt of democratic procedures, especially those of free speech, elections, and the open competition of ideas within the university itself. Tactics of civil disobedience have now been diffused internationally, and these are employed almost daily in battles within the universities. Vulnerable and apparently spineless, university authorities seem powerless to act, presumably because they cannot deal with anarchy and terror in a manner "befitting" their traditional educational role. Is it to be wondered that this growing civil disobedience should have so dramatically weakened, and in many cases ridiculed, the respect for the rule of law which guarantees the rights and the safety of all persons in all universities?

## Student Apathy and Academic Reform

At this point it is also necessary to stress that the success of terror and rising violence is to a large extent due to the receptivity which they have elicited in wide circles of society and government. Also, there can be no doubt that the increasing sense of grievance among the majority of students, and their consequent apathy toward anarchy, has heavily contributed to the rapid expansion of terror and chaos in our midst. For the time being, of course, the majority of students—the vast majority—are not revolutionaries. At worst they are apathetic and inactive. Nevertheless, these are two characteristics which greatly enhance the effectiveness of the eccentric and doctrinaire few—those devoted to violence and terror with a view to shattering the status quo. After all, what chance do the serious 90 per cent have in an environment where university authorities actually encourage the nonsense? As we shall see in Chapter 7, it may well be that "reform," and not overt revolution, is leading universities to disaster. Indeed, the worst possible effect of the actual violence of the few may well have been the unprecedented behavior it has elicited among the academic liberals. Were it not for this response the violence might not have been of real consequence to our universities. As the liberal academics go on feeding lawlessness, however, with their abortive crusades against all formal discipline, as the odd structure and existing policy of universities continue to make positive contributions to anarchy by inspiring a growing apathy among the majority of students, the time may not be so far off when all authority will be eroded and the destruction of universities as centers of learning will be complete.

## Changing Faculty Roles

For the reasons mentioned, the liberal academics may have systematically helped to create a climate of opinion which increases the apathy of the majority of students in the face of the terror of the few. But most students' unwillingness to come to the rescue of their universities also stems from changes in the role of the faculty. These changes have further contributed to making the situation of the student less attractive than it once was. As we have seen in Part One, with increasing size and greater pressures on faculty to do research, to publish, and to take part in extramural activities, poorer instruction, more faculty aloofness, and greater administrative indifference to students are beginning to take their toll. The research-oriented faculty increasingly gives a larger proportion of its limited teaching time to graduate students. Thanks to the arteriosclerotic financial structures of universities, university administration is almost exclusively involved in fund raising, lobbying public officials, handling of research contracts, or recruiting prestigious faculty. There can be little doubt that undergraduate students, as such, are of much less concern to the faculty and administration than in earlier periods. There can also be little doubt that many undergraduates have become apathetic in the face of the lethal dangers which now threaten their universities.

At the same time, the very increase in the importance of the university as a center of influence and power—indeed as the major accrediting institution of the society—has proportionately reduced the informal influence of students within the university. Still worse, the increased involvement of the faculty in a national and international prestige system (based on evaluations of their scholarly achievements or extramural activities), together with the sharp rise in their income (partly from extra-university employment), has meant that university teaching is no longer the fundamental aspect of being a university professor. Faculty members consequently find themselves in a highly competitive situation in which they are judged on the basis of their national and international celebrity ratings. Yet, by simple arithmetic, only a small share of any university's faculty can succeed in becoming nationally and internationally recognized figures. Most faculty turn out, by definition, to be failures in the supra-university struggle for scholarly status. Accompanying this depreciation of the teaching function as a source of economic reward and status is the obvious tendency of many disgruntled faculty members to ride the wave of student militancy against the forces which they hold responsible for their status inferiority or insecurity. Hence, many tend to advocate license for themselves and for students, instilling in the latter the views that they are neglected and misused by the administration, the trustees, other faculty, the society, the system.

## Theirs Not to Reason Why

With a fresh sense of anger flowing from their situation (a sense which is naturally best directed against the university), increasing numbers of students (and particularly those with a politically critical background) become yet more receptive to political action directed against trends in the larger society. As we have already suggested, students are more inclined to act than other groups—especially in the realm of politically oriented behavior. Young people have always been more available for new political movements than adults. In his excellent analysis of student activism, Seymour Lipset has also proposed that as new citizens, as people entering the political arena, students have no explicit commitments, are less tied to existing ideologies, are less identified with people or institutions which are responsible for the status quo, and have no previous personal positions to defend. Still worse, they know less recent history than adults. The key formative events in foreign or domestic policy, which usually spark off their imagination, are consequently appreciated in absolute, highly abstract, oversimplified, and largely irrelevant terms.

But students are also more available for activism because of the lesser commitments they have to their "occupational" role as compared to adults. They are increasingly capable of taking time off from work without suffering appreciable economic consequences. They are in the peculiar economic position of living on a relatively low income flow while at the same time anticipating a much higher income flow in postgraduation years. Only the relatively low income flow is affected by any temporary withdrawal of effort. Students are far more likely to be active than those who are otherwise constrained by the necessity of earning their living. Students have perhaps the most dispensable job requirements of all; they can easily drop in and out of universities, just as they can put off their studies for short or long periods, without paying much of a price. And, even so, opportunity cost is probably unknown to most students. It is also helpful to recall here that, compared to other groups, students have fewer responsibilities in the form of commitments to families and jobs. The physical situation of the university further facilitates student (faculty) political involvement by making it relatively easy to mobilize students who are already disposed to act politically. The campus is clearly the ideal place in which to find large numbers of people in a common situation. Many universities have over 30,000 students concentrated in a small area. New ideas which arise in response to given issues move most rapidly among students, and consequently find their maximum base of support there. Only a small percentage of these massive student bodies can produce a large demonstration. These are some of the factors, which have opened up the highly remunerative field of terrorist tactics, as we suggest in the next chapter.

Despite the sum total of these forces working against them, however, the majority of the students in all countries remain somehow or other triumphantly quiescent and moderate in their views and behavior. A Gallup Poll taken in 1968 in Great Britain among students at Cambridge and Sussex (two of the most "energetic" of English universities) concluded that only 5 per cent of the Cambridge and 6 per cent of the Sussex students thought violence desirable to student demonstrations. Although, at Sussex, 67 per cent said that peaceful demonstrations are useful, only 40 per cent had ever participated in any—whereas at Cambridge the number approving of the idea in the abstract exceeds the number of demonstrators by 50 per cent to 21 per cent. The other half of Cambridge and one-third of Sussex regard all student demonstrations as being harmful or inconsequential. According to national surveys of student opinion in the United States, taken by the Harris Poll in 1965 and the Gallup Poll in 1968, approximately one-fifth of the students have participated in civil rights or political activities

(17 per cent in 1964–1965, the year of the Berkeley revolt, and 20 per cent in 1967–1968, the year of the McCarthy and Kennedy campaigns). It is equally known that radical activist groups generally have tiny memberships. New Left Students for a Democratic Society (SDS) claims a total membership of about 30,000 out of a national student body of 7 million. A Harris Poll of American students, taken in the spring of 1968, estimates that there are only about 100,000 radical activists in the whole country. This means they are approximately 1 or 2 per cent of the college population. At the same time, opinion surveys throughout the world indicate that the vast majority of students remain unsympathetic toward radical doctrines and tactics.

What can this mean? The answer is simple. Thanks to the ever-rising thirst of the news and communications media for facile sensationalism, the revolting few in our midst are increasingly dominating the tone of many campuses. Still worse, they have come to play a major role in influencing politics everywhere. Perhaps, therefore, the time has come to ask whether a new era based on the ideal of excellence in terror has not already been inaugurated on this good earth.

 *All that is necessary for the forces of evil to win in the world is for enough good men to do nothing.*
Edmund Burke

# Chapter 6

# *The Economics of Violence*

We have discussed the modern university's structure, and we have explained why the equilibrium that was propped up by tradition has been so disturbed by a variety of shock waves. Here we take a different tack. We examine the *economic anatomy of terror*. The analysis provides a vital ingredient in our more comprehensive explanation of university chaos. In essence, we consider the productivity or efficiency of investment in violence.

The economist's proclivity is to look at all human behavior in terms of exchange or trade. In a general way, all behavior can be forced into an exchange setting, including sex, science, religion, art, economics, and violence. But precisely because it is so general, this approach yields relatively little explanatory value. It seems reasonable, therefore, to attempt some sort of classification of human behavior into separate categories.

# From Sex to Violence

We can think of our classification scheme as an array along a unidimensional spectrum. At the one extreme we can think of a situation where all parties secure benefits without costs to any party. At the other extreme, we can think of a situation where only one party secures benefits, and does so by imposing harm on others at the expense of some cost to itself. It is singular, and strange, that the alleged sins of modern society are often lumped under the single rubric "sex and violence" by reactionary and conservative critics. The singularity arises because these two forms of behavior lie at diametrically opposed ends of the spectrum that we suggest. Ideally considered, sex involves mutual cooperation between two parties with the aim of securing mutual benefits without costs to either party. In the post-pill paradise where fear and probability of pregnancy can be assumed away, the ideal perhaps comes close to realization. Almost all other forms of mutual cooperation that yield benefits to all parties require, at least initially, some cost to someone.

Violence stands at the other extreme of the spectrum. Here one party explicitly inflicts harm on other parties, with the sole aim of securing benefits to himself alone. The only exceptions here are masochist-sadist perversions, where even violence can become analogous to sex in its behavioral description. But these aside, violence is a one-sided exchange, one party suffers for another's gain. In between these extreme behavioral limits, from sex to violence, almost all of human social relationships are described—from mother love to mopery.

## Sex, Exchange, and Violence

For purposes of simplifying our exposition, we shall group behavior into three categories with the specific form under each being used as an abstract ideal-type illustration. We summarize these three ideal-types as follows:

1. *Sex*—an idealized form of behavior involving mutual or voluntary agreement of all parties, which results in net benefits to all parties, and which requires no cost outlay by any party to secure these mutual benefits.
2. *Exchange*—an idealized form of behavior involving mutual or voluntary agreement of all parties, which results in net benefits to all parties, and which requires some cost outlay on the part of all parties to secure these benefits.
3. *Violence*—an idealized form of behavior, which involves coercion of some parties by other parties, which results in expected net benefits to some parties only, which explicitly harms other parties, and which requires some cost outlay on the part of the initiating party in order to secure the expected benefits.

## The Economics of Violence

Several important differences among these three ideal-types of behavior (not unlike Kenneth Boulding's tripartite classification of behavior systems) may be noted briefly. Sex and exchange are mutual relationships, voluntarily entered into by all parties. Violence must involve more than one party, but it is unilateral in a behavioral sense. Both exchange and violence, as opposed to sex, require that the acting parties undergo some costs in order to secure the benefits that are promised. In ordinary exchange each trader gives up or sacrifices some good or service that he values for another good or service that he values more highly. The buyer gives up money for apples; the seller gives up apples for money. In the case of violence, the generator of the action must invest time and resources in securing the benefits that he seeks. He must expend energy in mugging his victim; he must spend costly time in casing the joints that he plans to hit. Still more important, he must suffer the costs that are represented by the probability of counterviolence or punishment, whether inflicted by the intended victim, other parties, or by society at large.

## The Costs and Benefits of Terror

Let us now look more carefully at the simple economics of violence, terror, or the threat thereof. For our purposes at this stage, there is no need to make distinctions among the various forms of coercive behavior. First, let us look at the "demand" for acts of violence or terror. Individuals are led to undertake these acts because they predict results which they value. The demand for acts of violence is, therefore, directly derived from the demand for and the evaluation of the end result that these acts are supposed to produce. This holds whether these results are measurable physical goods or money, as with ordinary theft, or a change in faculty retention policy, as with the University of Chicago occupation in February, 1969. The first law of demand, the economist's most important predictive tool, can be applied directly to the demand for violence by its potential perpetrators. If the costs of undertaking acts of terror, or of threatening to take such acts, are increased, there will be fewer acts demanded.

Costs of threats and acts of terror can be increased in several ways. We should surely predict a reduction in terrorist or criminal activity if the expected probability of capture, conviction, and punishment were increased. The same result could be insured by some increase in the probability that potential victims of intimidation or violence would strike back. All of this seems clear enough when examined dispassionately. But as we have noted with respect to university response mechanisms, there is a cancer-like sickness about which makes otherwise rational persons support grossly destabilizing reaction chains with the result that social systems are shifted further and further from, rather than toward, some reasonable equilibrium.

It is not our task here to discuss the simple economics of crime, as such. Interesting work in this area is currently being done by several economists, among them Gary Becker, William Landes, Simon Rottenberg, and Gordon

# The Economics of Violence

Tullock. Our objective is more limited. We want to concentrate on the violence and the terror that has disrupted universities throughout the world in the late 1960's, from Japan to California via the Atlantic Ocean. The question we seek to answer is why has terror been so much more effective in this part of modern society than in others. Why have the universities and colleges been particularly vulnerable?

Many of the relevant ingredients for a proper answer have already been discussed in some detail. But we can now place these in a somewhat better perspective. The costs that the perpetrator of violence, the terrorist, must consider include both the expected probability of being captured, convicted, and punished along with the severity of the sentence, and the expected probability that his potential victims will strike back with the resources and power at their command. Both of these costs tend to be lower in the university setting than almost anywhere else in our society, and for reasons we have already noted.

## Costs Imposed by Probable Counterattack

Let us first consider the second of these cost items, summarized in the expected value of the probability that the potential victims will reciprocate and impose costs on the attacker. But who is really the target of the terror tactics that we have come to associate with campus chaos? Relatively few persons have been subjected to serious physical injury, and damage to life itself so far tends to be minimal in the sort of terror under discussion. Although physical destruction has been widespread, the tactics have generally been those which involve occupation and invasion of university property and the exclusion of others from the usage of this property. But whose property is being invaded and occupied? As we have shown in Chapter 4, the university structure is notoriously fuzzy as to its delineation of rights. Also, even where long-established rights seem to be violated (as, for example, in the case of the rights of professors to use their own offices), the "owners" do not possess personally marketable assets. Hence, so long as the university terrorists confine their action to these relatively limited forms of coercive behavior, the danger of effective retaliation on the part of faculties and university administrators is small. Experience has amply demonstrated this truth.

Faculties and administrations can, of course, penalize the terrorists without taking overt physical action. The faculty member need not clean out his office with a shotgun. Faculties can, if they so choose, modify rules on admissions and on retention which will make even the slightest violence or threat of violence extremely costly to the perpetrator. Even when we fully understand the vulnerability of the modern university, there must remain the question of why faculties and administrations have not been more severe in imposing additional costs on those militants who have been the source of the campus disruptions. It would seem possible to do with little or no apparent cost to those responsible for university decisions and rules. A set of para-economic explanations for this behavior was offered in the preceding chapter.

# The Economics of Violence

Economics yields only one part of the answer. To the extent that those who have initiated the limited violence have been successful in convincing the decision-makers that more severe action would have taken place in the event of a stiffening of penalties, the decision-makers have found their own costs significantly increased. There seems no doubt but that this threat of greater terror has inhibited faculty and administration response—and thus partially accounts for their highly insensitive behavior. So long as the overt acts of terror are sufficient to make threats of further acts creditable, the university staff which stands firm must bear significant costs in some expected value sense. This is, of course, precisely the state of mind that the terrorist seeks in his opponents. If he can succeed in making his threat of potential violence fully creditable, he may secure his objectives without overt acts against either person or property. And this will obviously be a more efficient means than the *actual* carrying out of overt acts. As George Orwell remarked, the best trained dog is the one which responds without the whip being cracked. University faculties in the late 1960's often resemble such trained dogs, responding to potential terror in absurd ways even before the threats could possibly have been considered real.

But this is not enough. For a fuller explanation of the collective passivity of university-college decision-makers in the face of campus militancy, we must go beyond the simple economics. Clearly, the ideological biases of modern university faculties involve, in general, certain prejudices about social organization and, in particular, the apparent guilt com-

dicted responses to economic stimuli. Those who commit the overt acts of violence and who threaten further acts are no different in this respect from others. We reject the view that classifies these persons as deviants, as psychopaths, whose behavior is simply beyond the realm of rational explanation, economic or otherwise. The behavior of the activist student militant may seem bizarre, even insane, to the man who consistently holds wholly differing value standards. But differences in value priorities do not imply that economic motivation is present under one set of values and not under another. Although his hair might still be significantly longer than our own, the hippie would himself have shorter hair if a tax on hair length should be levied.

Why does the student activist act? He acts, presumably, because he wants to see certain objectives secured. The militant acts because he wants certain things to happen which would not happen without his acting. This does not say much. But it does get us started to think rationally about what may seem to be irrational behavior. In many cases, of course, the militant acts for the sense of involvement itself—for the "happening" that acting represents. In this case, his behavior is akin to the one who supports education for its own sake, discussed in some detail in Chapter 4. But, for now, let us consider the militant who undertakes an illegal act of violence against university property with a specific objective in view. He smashes a window, throws a Molotov cocktail, invades a building, occupies a professor's office, and so forth. He does this because he predicts that, as a result of his doing so, some objective will be furthered. And the advantages that he expects to result must be sufficient to offset the costs that he incurs by taking the action.

## Moral Principle as a Cost

An overly simplistic economic approach to the cost-benefit calculus of the terrorist would conceal important behavioral influences which add to the explanation of the peculiar locational incidence of university chaos. The militant terrorist probably secures no pleasure from the destruction of property or inflicted harm to persons as such. This seems to us to be a relatively important and critical factor. If the activist should be totally disinterested in the preservation of the property and lives of others than his own group, he would always make the simple cost-benefit calculation we have suggested above. And, so long as expected benefits exceed expected costs, he would act. It is as simple as that. But destruction and harm to others, either to property or persons, is not desired as such. In fact, it is disagreeable to many persons, probably to almost all. Ingrained in Western tradition is a sense of respect for the rights of others, including property rights. It becomes, therefore, costly for the person deliberately to undertake action that he knows will destroy property and perhaps life. Such wanton destruction and harm may be recognized as means of securing the objectives that he seeks. But there are moral precepts which exist, for the activist as well as for the nonactivist, and these can be translated into economic terms. And to the extent that the activist has such precepts, the cost side of his choice is more heavily weighted than simplistic cost-benefit accounting might suggest. He may have to overcome moral principle before embarking on action that involves destruction to property and harm to others. The existence of such moral principle seems more likely to be relevant in inhibiting behavior in Western than in Eastern cultures. This, in itself, may provide a partial explanation of the relative severity of student riots in Japan.

Temptation is strong to extend this discussion beyond the limits of economics, even when quite literally interpreted. Ethical rules lend themselves readily to such expanded discourse. Nevertheless, only one question need be asked. Is there not general agreement that the strength of moral precept in inhibiting individual behavior has become progressively weaker through time? If this is accepted, we can state unequivocably that one element in the cost of the potential terrorist has been falling progressively through time. We witness the university chaos of the 1960's. What does this portend for 1984?

Activists who are at all bothered with moral or ethical principle will be more likely to strike at places where principle is less inhibiting. Again the university becomes the ideal target, and for reasons already noted several times. The student who throws the brick is not aiming at some person's home. He is hitting property that belongs to everyone in general and, because of this very fact, to no one in particular. The effect of commonality on behavior and on attitudes toward behavior is universally recognized and empirically supported. Corroboration of this point was provided by events at the University of Chicago in early 1969. The faculty remained unenthusiastic about the punishment of militants who invaded the administration building. This same faculty supported effective disciplinary measures when the president's home (still university property) became the target.

The professional revolutionaries whose agitation is increasingly tolerated by modern society recognize all of this. They recognize that the potential student activists whose support is essential have morality thresholds which must be surmounted before they can be induced to take action. This is why the revolutionaries first depersonalize the targets selected for attack. The "people's park" upheaval in Berkeley in May, 1969 adequately illustrates the point. Common property is always inviting (and the university doubly so) since the raw student can be convinced that here, after all, he does have some "rights" that have been trampled on. This is especially likely to be the case if the facility embodies no scarcity value to the student. The professional revolutionary supplements and feeds the depersonalization by making the potential terrorist adopt group, class, or race enemies. If the activist can become convinced that the cops (better known as the "campus pigs"), the establishment, the power structure, or "the honkies" are his enemies—easy stereotypes to be effectively despised—his morality threshold may practically vanish. Adherence to common standards of morality is probably a much more important cementing influence in modern society than we are wont to acknowledge, and its elimination may produce highly unpleasant consequences. Guilt by association, by class or group affiliation—this is the order of the day in modern university militant discourse and action. On this new guilt by association as a technique, many faculty members are strangely silent. These men, who were so openly and stridently vocal during the McCarthyism of the early 1950's, seem to be revealed as those for whom it is forever wrong to be right and almost always right to be left.

## The Judgment of Peers

We should be remiss in our survey of the costs and benefits that the militant activist faces if we did not again emphasize the relevance of the attitude of the great and silent majority of students. All accounts of the university crises that have occurred point up the fact that the disruption and destruction is carried out by a tiny minority of students. Why is it possible for a small minority to disrupt the operations of a university that numbers its students in the thousands? Why could an activist group estimated at 30 students close down the London School of Economics for a lengthy period in early 1969, a mere 1 per cent of the total student body of 3,000? Why could a mere 300 students, less than 2 per cent of the 18,000 enrolled, effectively disrupt San Francisco State College for most of the 1968–1969 academic year? We have already discussed the para-economics of the phenomenon.

Once again we can identify the problem in economic

terms. The dissident, the militant, surely counts the predicted or probable reaction of his peers as one of the costs that he faces. He may not reckon on specific counteraction, but he will think twice before proceeding boldly in open opposition to what the great masses of students want. Social sanctions are strong medicine, in any group, and students are no different from another. Witness the rare student who chose not to be eccentric in dress and hair style on a University of California campus in 1969. The significant fact is that, despite the small minority of activists, the great majority of students has not actively opposed the terror tactics of the militants. This is far more important than the converse statement that these students do not support the terror. Failure of support and failure of opposition are not the same. There is a wide threshold in between, and this should also be recognized.

We must ask why the majority does not oppose the minority? Clearly, the terror tactics impose costs on students. Under any reasonable cost-benefit calculations, and given the way universities are now organized, the students who find their educational processes disrupted are the main losers from the chaos that is visited on the campuses. This must be felt by the students themselves. Why, then, do they submit, why do they acquiesce? Fear itself may be of some explanatory value, but this does not seem to be the main answer. More important reasons have already been suggested. Basically, students lack a sufficient stake in the structure of the university. The system is not geared to their own demands. Universities and colleges are not responsive to their needs, nor are they felt to be responsive. In fact, there are no effectively competing universities among which the student may select his own preferred product qualities. He, therefore, feels barred from satisfying his own objectives, as best he knows them.

When the militants thrust their way upon the scene, the student vaguely senses that he is the big loser. But he sees more clearly that the militants' objective is to force change on the university, change which in its specifics he may not prefer, but change nonetheless. The majority of students are willing to watch from the sidelines, so to speak, and if the university responds in manners which violate some sense of "hair play" (that is, fair play), or what propagandists make one think to be this sense, many students become willing to lend a hand to the dissidents—if only via their apathy.

## The Tactics of Violence

The university has been revealed as a soft underbelly of modern society, and its attractiveness to the revolutionary sharks is evident. We have not, to this point, discussed explicitly the tactics of disruption within the university itself. At what points of the structure and at what times, where and when, can we predict the outbreaks of violence?

The pattern is familiar. The targets within the university are selected in precisely the same way that the university itself is selected. The professional revolutionary searches out and finds the soft spots in a structure that is full of them. There is no need to discuss in detail the manner in which the attempt is made to seek out and find issues that can command the assent of large numbers of nonmilitants, to wait until "legitimate" grievances appear, and then lend support to those who are seeking it. The strategy is to be found in the revolutionists' handbooks which now circulate freely on our campuses. With such flexibility, we should predict that, generally speaking, the issues would vary from time to time, and from one country to another. In many cases, the decisive issues turn out to be something quite specific to a single campus.

## The American Tragedy of Race

In American universities and colleges, however, one issue has dominated much of the chaos. Although some of the critical confrontations have not been explicitly racial (for example, Berkeley in 1964, Columbia in 1969), the great majority of American university troubles in the period 1964–1970 exhibited racial overtones. The alleged treatment of racial minorities, among students, faculties, and communities at large, provides a common theme and set of issues running through the whole university scene in the United States.

Unfortunately, this pattern is explained perfectly by the strategy we have sketched. Apparently a great majority of white Americans harbor a guilt complex about the treatment accorded the Negro throughout most of the nation's history. This seems to have become an overwhelming consensus in the ranks of the academic liberals who dominate university and college faculties. Because of this apparent guilt complex, faculties appear peculiarly vulnerable to the demands placed upon them by black students or on behalf of black students. The revolutionary adopts the black students as his most attractive allies. He encourages and supports black student movements even in absurd demands in the knowledge that, at best, faculty-administration response will be embarrassed, slow, and confused. Interestingly, militant groups have found that their usage of black students is sometimes far too successful. Universities have often been so willing to yield to the demands made upon them by black student groups that the militants have found it difficult to produce the confrontation that they seek. To the extent that black students can be placed in the forefront of the militants' ranks, two reactions are guaranteed. First, the response of the authorities will tend to be much less vigorous. (The intensity of the response of the Chicago police in August, 1968 is widely attributed to the fact that the demonstrators were white.) And, second, if the authorities, either within the university or without, are provoked into responding, the sympathy of nonactivist students and faculty members is much more likely to be aroused.

If we translate this into the cost-benefit calculus facing the university decision-makers, the guilt complex amounts to a serious cost barrier that inhibits effective retaliatory action. In this setting, as well as in many others in modern American society, the developing pattern has all of the characteristics of a Greek tragedy. The genuine American liberal finds himself unable to act so as to prevent what he can foresee as a tragic unfolding of events.

Compounding the racial issues, but much less important than these in America, is the fact that university faculties are dominated by those who share what can be classified as a left-liberal ideology. This is also recognized by the professional revolutionary, and modern university disruptions are almost always mounted from the left rather than from the right. If you have any doubt as to the validity of the discussion of the previous few paragraphs, try to imagine what might have happened at any American university if the same number of militants had done precisely the same things at the same time—but with only one difference. Imagine what might have happened if these students should have been supporters of George Wallace instead of the Black Students' Union or the Students for a Democratic Society. Reaction would have been total, swift, and severe.

## Rewards and Punishments

The simple economics of terror, once understood, leads directly to the political economy of its control. If violence and threat of violence are things to be reduced in the social interest, economics points directly toward remedial steps that can be taken. These apply whether we are referring to the university or to the wider world beyond. The costs to those who would seek benefits through coercion must

## The Economics of Violence

be increased, and the costs to those who would react against violence should be reduced. Or, on the benefit side, the expected gains to those who would perpetrate violence on others must be reduced, while the expected gains to those who might stop the terror should be increased. These are simple and elementary principles. Almost everyone recognizes their validity. If social policy, in the university and beyond, should have been consistently based on these principles, this little book need not have been written.

*Many of you have told me that in most parts of the campus one is unaware that a "strike" is going on. . . . The theory, as explained by one of the leaders, is to increase slowly the violence and terror of students, faculty and administrators, so that they will eventually be willing to sue for peace. It starts with blocking pedestrians and turning in false alarms—there were eight in the first few days of the strike—and then moves on to fires and fire-bombs. There have been seven attempts at arson or fire-bombing to this date. We have stopped counting bomb threats; there have been four battery complaints; there have been many threats on the lives of students and faculty and at least one faculty member has been knocked down. As of last week a total of 14 buildings have had some damage and several classes have been disrupted. Let there be no mistake about the phenomenon we are dealing with, or of the intentions of some of those making the operating decisions . . .*

Chancellor Roger Heyns,
University of California, Berkeley,
February 3, 1969.

# Chapter 7

# *The Strategy of Terror*

Gustav Fechner's one-hundred-year-old fantasy that sensations increase in arithmetical progression while corresponding stimuli increase in geometrical progression remains a useful relic. As a strictly scientific proposition, the statement is not valid. It has nevertheless had its uses. The widely accepted view that human behavior is always characterized by threshold-sensitive, as opposed to hypersensitive, response to the stimuli produced by our environment stems directly from it. A certain threshold has to be crossed or "saturated" before human response to the excitational stimuli of our environment can be seen to take place. We have already touched upon several instances of this central truth. We shall see that this same phenomenon lies at the heart of the strategy of terror in modern academia.

Nonacademic illustrations are manifold. For example, unless a joke produces some minimum intensity of "funniness" no one laughs; just as we would not normally begin to weep before "painfulness" overcomes a certain range of insensitivity which generally protects our composure. Some people scream at the mere sight of a dentist's drill. But they are exceptions to the rule—and few would take them seriously. The opposite case is more familiar, where we would expect but do not observe complaints. Nor should one have to be reminded here of Indian fakirs lying in apparently blissful tranquility on their beds of nails. The truth of the matter is simpler.

Before acting or reacting—behaving—we saturate our thresholds. They are there to assist. They are life's own shock absorbers. They prevent us from behaving explosively, hypersensitively—ludicrously. Not every imperfection or departure from normality in our environment is capable of eliciting a response. Were this not so, the world would have long ago ceased to exist. It would have exploded in a cumulative frenzy of hyperactivity. Fortunately, a vast complex of thresholds, or positive ranges of insensitivity or indifference, must first be overcome before environmental stimulation is able to trigger any reportable human response. Everyday experience easily confirms this axiom.

## Terror, Thresholds, and Reform

What we have summarized is a fundamental property which characterizes both individual and group behavior. It is not difficult to see at once how some of its consequences can be helpful in explaining—and, if properly understood, critical in influencing—the world around us, including the universe of the academe. In fact, both student activists and the faculty-administrator liberal reformers seem—intuitively at least—to be well versed in the intricacies of threshold-sensitive responses. Both seem aware that a twofold proposition of strategic value follows from the threshold-sensitive stimulus-response model of human behavior. Let us quickly run through the sequence.

First, is it not evident that with an adequate technique of manipulating selected threshold limits upwards, or discriminately working their way with existing ones, unpopular, undesirable, even criminal activities could be made to pass relatively unnoticed? The converse also holds, of course, and its implications are no less significant. For it is equally true that by causing selected thresholds to shrink, and in turn concentrating on oversensitive sectors in the environment, desired results (by way of expected responses) can be realized with a minimum stimulatory thrust. The applicability of this two-tier strategic orientation is universal. It relates to the descriptive, prescriptive, and preventive aspects of all human policy—whether in war or peace. It sheds some light on university chaos today, if only because of the curious mix of war and peace that characterizes life in contemporary academia. As Peter Bauer has recently suggested to us, conditions prevailing in most universities today can probably be best explained as resembling a state of undeclared civil war. This is important, as we suggest below.

## The Strategy of Terror

Continuing with the simple sequence involved here, we may begin with the outlook of student terrorism. The exercise of student terror forces existing thresholds in certain directions to shrink. By concentrating on sufficiently oversensitive sectors in the academic milieu, desired results can be realized with a minimum stimulatory thrust. As we have seen in the preceding chapter, an elementary cost-benefit interpretation of terror suggests that its marginal efficiency is inversely related to the marginal costs of terrorist activity. It follows that the more sensitive the environment where terror is applied, the less intense the required thrust. The lower the thrust, the lower the cost, and thus the higher the expected value of the venture. But *whose* thresholds will those under attack or "cultivation" be?

Naturally, the relevant targets here are the tolerance limits of the academic liberal. He is being continuously "manipulated" so that at some desired stage he begins to respond almost hypersensitively to every successive act of violence. At the same time, it is imperative to realize that the principle of creeping advance is strictly applied. Success and gradualness are here inexorably bound together. In fact, this seems to be the creed of all those addicted to terror. Civil war remains always undeclared. Student activism very rarely erupts into a total, all-out confrontation. All attacks are limited. Whether advertised or realized, arson and firebombing, sit-ins and assassinations, strikes and invasions—these are invariably limited, calculated, optimally restrained activities. With few exceptions, all advances are so designed as to work discriminately within the operational thresholds of the majority and hence pass relatively unnoticed for certain carefully selected critical periods and directions. Celebrated by now, the well-known technique has always been to increase demands gradually—so that, eventually, when it appears that the administration cannot grant any one of them, the standard outcry against it can be heard. Its "bourgeois," "repressive" nature can then be exposed to the multitudes. And what could possibly emerge as more obvious than the call that so odious a seat of corruption must at long last be annihilated?

Two consequences are predictably apparent in this process. On the one hand, the receptivity of the majority of students is affected to the advantage of the terrorists. Most students tend to become so conditioned, and their tolerance limits so enlarged, that further terrorist activity can be "sheltered"—that is, insured against any noticeable reaction from the student body at large. The nature of the motivation of both the average student and the terrorist is important here, as we have already suggested. On the other hand, every additional step in student violence is so calculated as to push increasing numbers of academic liberals into ever greater sprees of activity masquerading under the usual reform euphemisms. Delicately working its way through existing threshold-sensitivities, modern terror thus succeeds in accomplishing two objectives at once: it gradually increases the tolerance of the majority of students, while at the same time it diminishes the response inertia of carefully selected minorities among teaching and administrative staff. In brief, the sensitivity of the latter rises at the expense of a predictably declining willingness to respond to violence and terror among the former. The validity of this observation has been widely demonstrated. The newly acquired responsiveness of most universities to the stimuli (whether overtly insane or not) flowing from the violence and terror of the few bears solemn testimony to this end. Less and less sensitive to the (dull and unsophisticated?) behavior of the majority of students, universities have become almost exclusively responsive—and hypersensitively at that—to the mean anarchy of the few. At the mercy of those who are addicted to physical and intellectual vandalism, many of our colleges and universities have gradually limited themselves to one single option: an agonizing ride to the unknown.

This brings us to the role played by the liberal academician. At first it appears difficult to choose between two competing hypotheses about the motivation behind his actual behavior. He may be hopelessly naive in his reading of human nature, so much so that he leaves himself open to the grossest exploitation by the terrorists. Or, conversely, he may be quite sophisticated in masking his genuine objectives in the liberal cloth, and in so doing quite successfully exploiting those of his fellows who accept his statements of intent at face value. Perhaps there are both sorts about, and perhaps each academic liberal is really a different blend of these disparate species. For predictive purposes, however, this does not matter. As he is observed to act, the academic liberal seems to behave on the standard motto that, little by little, small changes can wreck established institutions. He takes the baton, in fact, just as his terrorist "predecessors" pass it to him. In principle, oversensitive to the frightening mix of villainy and intelligence of the anarchic few—their "baby," so to speak—he oozes with passions and desires to change and reform everything in sight. Let some departmental offices be invaded and the chairman be held captive for a few days or his life threatened at gunpoint. A new body of formal studies will result—invariably concentrating on research on the ethnic history and culture of the invaders, often topped by a special admissions program to make certain that more of the same will soon be around. For behind every new act of terror mounted from the left, the liberal in our midst sees, or claims that he sees, a condition of injustice. Following every act of violence, he seeks to appease. It seems to become his guilty responsibility to put all right. And further inspired by the violence he himself helps to escalate, he strives to take a firmer stand against all discipline. His is the job of feeding violence with concession.

Like his sophisticated terrorist protégés, however, he is not stupid. He senses that where blatant revolution fails, creeping reform is triumphant. He would be the first to acknowledge that the recent French experience epitomizes this truth. When 10 per cent of the student population flagrantly revolted in Paris in May, 1968 against de Gaulle's France—and society's thresholds were everywhere smashed—the people as a whole rose in anger. And with one sweeping electoral blow, the Old Man's ways were suddenly restored—at least for a year.

## The Strategy of Terror

Calm and contained, therefore, the academic liberal provokes little opposition—and, where he has to, only such as is equally cool and compromising. Everywhere manipulating selected thresholds, and carefully operating within existing ranges of inertia, his method works wonders. Things are changed a little at a time, the right time, in the left direction. Hypersensitive to every act of vandalism, he carefully records all manifestations of terror deep in his heart. His will to reform may be total, his commitment to "overwhelm" violence with concession absolute, but his action is, must be, always limited. Without the basic transformation ever being forced on everyone's attention, therefore, our universities are being fundamentally undermined. The activity is feverish. It goes on and on, but always beneath the surface, where it cannot be perceived at first. And as the community's thresholds are consequently expanded, more and more elbowroom becomes available. More and more people can see less and less, even though all can feel that life is changing faster than before. It all seems to be much like the two arms of a big clock. Neither must ever move along too abruptly or too fast in order to go on telling us the truth about the changing time, all the time. Of course, the clock runs in a perfect, predictable, cycle. The path is certain; no surprises exist. Unfortunately, the same cannot quite be said of the "subterranean" activism of the liberal reformer. As the durability of our institutions is continuously being eroded, it is impossible to know precisely where we are heading.

But supposing reform has its way (as it probably will).

What will change produce? Supported by the inertia of the many, ignited by the terror of the few, and injected into our lives via the ever-so-gentle touch of the academic liberal —how will change of this sort affect the modern university? Could it be that degrees by popular acclaim is the surprise we can all expect?

## Graduation by Popular Acclaim

Once upon a time, we are told, universities were voluntary associations of learning which rested on mutual consent for the reasoned exploration and advancement of knowledge. Universities were institutions where two basically unequal communities met in harmony. A set of relatively immature or less adequately educated persons— known as students—willingly presented themselves for a certain period of time to a more adequately educated set of persons—known as the faculty—in order to experience a personal transformation process leading to the acquisition of superior knowledge and reasoning power. Academic freedom in such halcyon days meant freedom to teach and freedom to learn within an ordered framework of rational behavior and natural Socratic authority, infused over the years with the privilege of free speech and constructive dissension. Any explicit violation of so sacred a constitutional framework, held together by a set of implicitly accepted behavioral rules, over and above the written bylaws, was treated with a mixture of pity and contempt reserved for the vulgar everywhere. The university functioned with many of the characteristics of a Gentlemen's Club, and it required mutual adherence of its various members to agreed behavioral standards for its very existence. In this same golden age, direct university participation in society's current political or social turmoil was seldom viewed as an appropriate, and certainly not as a necessary, activity. Neither the less nor the more adequately educated members of the university community felt that the fundamental function of the academic world, the learning process, would stand to benefit by moral commitments to this or to that social or political cause which current developments in the national or the international scene might warrant. Although this particular "law" had (like many others) remained an unwritten one for generations, the convention was solidly established that *only* by remaining apolitical houses of study, could universities best serve, first, man's natural impulse to go on improving his individual knowledge and ameliorating his judgment and, second, society's long-term process via the systematic increase in the number of those whose actions might be governed by reason.

Then, of course, came the confrontation of the 1960's. And, as we write, the whole constitutional framework of the university is in the process of being challenged. Its methods are criticized as archaic and its noncommittal role is condemned. *Relevance*, in principle, has become the watchword of liberal reform, and change has certainly come upon us. But what kind?

The dedicated efforts of the violent few among the body of students have been brought into early fruition. Thanks, also, to the farseeing crusades of the academic liberals in our faculties, constitutional authority is everywhere massively retreating. By virtue of an immaculately camouflaged disregard of ordered processes of change, based on modern terror's impressive understanding of the dynamics of threshold-sensitively linked human interrelations, modern universities have been inexorably caught in a whirlwind of uncontrolled change. Deeply committed grouplets of students contemptuous themselves of democratic procedures —especially those of free speech, free elections, and the open competition of ideas within the university itself—are rapidly converting academia into a battleground where the employment of physical force has become a compensatory prerequisite for the dissemination of intellectually impoverished ideas.

A wealth of examples comes to mind. Events from Berkeley, Berlin, London, Rome, Paris, or Tokyo are all too well known to merit repetition. One or two less celebrated scenes might be yet more helpful—especially to the initiated. As William Letwin relates, at the University of Leeds students insulted, jostled, and tripped the wife of a Conservative Member of Parliament as she left a lecture he had just delivered. The message she grasped was clear enough. "Never come back—or else." At the University of Exeter, students prevented a lecture from being given on a scientific subject by a doctor of sciences who had the distinct misfortune to work at the British Government's research center on warfare. When the (three) leaders of the demonstration were suspended from the university, a week of sit-ins, sleep-ins, teach-ins, and general abandonment of academic work followed, until the vice-chancellor's ruling was properly reversed by a majority of the faculty led by (three) young teachers. As soon as the rebels were welcomed back to the fold, the announcement followed: "We have demonstrated what is fundamentally wrong with the university—that it is a power structure run by a small oligarchical group who dictate conditions. What we want is a genuine democratic university run jointly by students and staff." Both the syllogism in itself and the context of its presentation stuns the mind of the sane—especially if one considers that the usual reference to the necessary inclusion of the kitchen staff in the "democratization" of the academia was this time only inadvertently omitted. As everyone knows, it is almost universally conceded that the university cannot deal with this kind of onslaught in a manner befitting its educational or gentlemanly character. So the massive retreat goes on.

Where will this lead us? Can the progressive "democratization" of the university, which is increasingly in the air, be a good thing? As more and more "paternalistic" rules and regulations, whether written or unwritten, are abolished; as freedom to teach and freedom to learn gradually lose their natural balance inspired by the Socratic ideal; as activist student evaluation of teaching performance spreads; as their participation in university policy further expands; as their voice in the selection and promotion of faculty and administration becomes more decisive; as such students themselves gradually acquire a say in the final assessment of academic performance; and as the university is at last so reoriented as to become an integral part of the general social and political controversies confronting society at large—what lies ahead? In particular, where student-consumers do not behave as economic adults within an educational-market framework activated by competitively determined checks and balances, such as we discussed in Part One, is it possible that terrorist-consumer sovereignty in the educational process can be the ideal?

Furthermore, is there any reason to expect that the dramatic changes taking place can be, or should be, confined to the university-college level? The wave of terror that swept the secondary schools in many American cities in 1969 suggests that there is no sharp dividing line between the school and the university. And, even if activist student sovereignty is acknowledged to merit some attention at the college-university level, can this be extended lower and lower down the educational ladder? Perhaps some insight into one ultimate source of all our difficulties is offered by such an extension as this. As children in kindergarten become sovereign over their instruction and instructors, do we not properly raise the next question? Should not pre-school children also be allowed full rights of participation and determination of the relevancy of instruction? Surprisingly, this is the gospel of the permissiveness of the modern era. So, after all, the whole notion of imposed standards and discipline throughout the educational process, from kindergarten through the university, may be anachronistic. If small children are allowed to be anarchists, should large children be treated any differently?

At this point we should naturally pause to emphasize one very important difference between consumer sovereignty in a market order and voter sovereignty in a political order—a difference that extends with vengeance to the parallels in the educational structure. Buyer-consumers in a market are "sovereign" because they *indirectly* determine the allocation of economic resources by their choices among *competing* uses. Translated into everyday language, the housewife determines whether or not the corner grocery store will be prosperous by her willingness to shop there. Her selection among alternative sources of supply indirectly determines who shall be prosperous. The specific corner grocery may not survive, but the housewife continues to face many retail outlets. The sovereignty of the consumer does not result in the selection of a single monopoly retail outlet in the community. In relatively sharp contrast with this, voter sovereignty in political democracy normally produces a single result. Only one candidate or one party can be in office at a time, and those in the opposing minority have no option but to abide by the wishes of the majority.

Let us quickly apply this to the university scene. Student-consumers in an educational-market framework would have the opportunity to select from among alternative universities; and, by their choices, they would be able *indirectly* to exert control over the form and content of university programs. On the other hand, even if student-consumers should be granted something akin to full voter sovereignty *within* a single monopoly structure, each of them could secure, at best, only one single voice in determining a program that, once chosen, must be applied to all. As compared with genuine student-consumer control in a market structure, therefore, any participatory democracy comes off a very poor second best—from the students' own point of view in particular. If, however, the participatory democracy is only apparent, if students are not allowed equal voices in the determination of policy within a monolithic university structure, if the student-terrorists really become sovereign, then the general student-consumer is in the worst of all possible worlds. This is true even if we should ignore the interests and values of everyone else involved in the educational process.

Can this then be the road to a better university world? Time will judge. Who knows, perhaps the delicately managed gradualness with which the "democratization" of academia is taking place is in tune with the future. After all, innovation is based on forward, not backward, adjustments. Perhaps it *was* preposterous to have assumed for so long that we are not *all* equals in the academic world. Perhaps even Plato was wrong in setting out to develop a definition of justice based upon inequalities among men—which he, too, felt were continuously varying with alternative states of the world in time and in space. Instead of merely being free to judge whether or not they are enjoying the business of learning—or, instead, to repeat an obvious alternative, of being given the power to shop around for varying educational processes regulated by the internal dynamics of an adequately competitive seller's market—terrorist-controlled students should perhaps reign supreme in academia. Technically, this is easy. The community of terrorist-influenced students within any university would vastly outnumber and outman those in any coalition of teaching-administration-and-kitchen staff. Perhaps William Letwin was out of his wits when he wrote that student-dominated university democracy is as reasonable a thing as a piece of marble telling the sculptor how to carve —or, say, arguing that everyone's theater-going habits should be so readjusted so that the audience should tell the actors how to perform.

One thing, of course, should be clear. The momentum of student unrest is bound to go on growing. And, as long as no alternative equilibrium mechanism is forthcoming, the "democratization" of our universities may well increase until the rule of adolescence is absolute. Perhaps this is the will of God. We have already seen that our culture has been preparing us for the ultimate in this Era of Neolatry. To paraphrase Shakespeare somewhat, perhaps the *Marseillaise* of the 1970's will be sung to the words, "If youth be the food of progress, carry on! Sit-in, teach-in, love-in, give us excess of it!" It is already standard procedure in totalitarian countries that official student organizations should be the political arm of the (permanently) ruling party. Will it be long before students in the West will be dictating the conclusions their teachers should reach, especially on important and controversial matters? Under the felicitous slogans of "student rights" and "participatory democracy," and thanks to the rising number of enlightened liberal academics in our midst, perhaps we can all look forward to an early new understanding of academic freedom—that is, universities efficiently dropping or adding teaching or research activities in whatever fields the student body at large deems fit for academic enquiry and investigation.

Nor, while we are in this trance, should we forget how "fortunate" we are that our community, thanks to the concerted efforts of the anarchic few among us, has been spared the clash of force with force, how "fortunate" that our citadels of reason have been saved the tragedy of having to declare their undeclared civil war. We have proved magnificently successful, we are often told, in having forestalled "overreaction" to the violence of the few. But we have, of course, carefully deplored in advance the potential corrective action of the many—which would have been required to substitute intellectual for physical power in our universities. As Sydney Hook has nostalgically reminisced, there have always been extremists in academic life. But they had always remained peripheral or atrophic grouplets moving in harmlessly eccentric orbits. All of this has changed in more recent times. Gentlemenly dissension has become a thing of the past. The Violence and Terror Noise Duet, basing its success on the golden rule that carefully managed small hits can ultimately wreck great barriers, is today's Tops of the University Pops. Extremist students have at last discovered the tricks required in order to metamorphose themselves into a noise capable of paralyzing great centers of learning such as the London School of Economics or the Sorbonne, among others. It remains to be seen whether the grandest, and possibly the last, song of the Neolatres will in fact prove to be Graduation by Popular Acclaim.

*Selected almost at random*
   Albany, N.Y.
   BLACK STUDENTS WIN COURSE DEMANDS

(*Associated Press*) *The Black Students Alliance has won approval to form an Afro-American studies department at the State University of New York here next fall.*

*The student group had said earlier that it was "ready to take any means necessary" to obtain affirmation of its demands.*

*Dr. Evan R. Collins, the university's president, agreed to all the demands made by a nine-member alliance committee.*

*The alliance called for:*

   *Institution of an Afro-American history course during the coming spring semester.*

   *The enrollment next fall of at least 300 more non-white students at the university.*

   *The right to play a decisive role in both the recruiting and screening of all potential instructors and in the structuring of the department's curriculum.*

   *The right to participate in the recruiting of non-white students.*

   *Dr. Collins said that although he was disappointed that the student group presented a list of demands, rather than making a proposal, he felt all the demands were reasonable and fit in with the current thinking of the university.*

                              *The Christian Science Monitor,*
                              February 14, 1969

# Chapter 8

# *Prediction and Prophecy*

During the Great Depression of the 1930's it was said that "the study of economics won't keep you out of the bread-line—but at least you will know why you're there." Something very similar is applicable here. The economic vision of university chaos will hardly tell you how to transform the beast into a beauty. But it may help to understand why the sometimes cozy world of academia now festers with ugliness. Still more important, and more hopefully, it may allow some glimpses into alternative futures, some of which are not necessarily shrouded in gloom. Drowsy scholars and dusty dons alike seem to be awakening in recognition of the university destruction that is proceeding apace. We are past the stage where only the small boy is shouting that the king has no clothes. Those learned fools who mouth absurdities in their fear-racked, guilt-ridden response to overt terror are being increasingly called to account. And contempt rises for those academicians who

But all things come at a cost. And the educational establishment is learning rapidly that there are no free lunches after all. Precisely because of the uniform image, which the public holds rightly or wrongly, the riot on a single campus sheds its blight on all. The arson at Berkeley burns a bit of Vanderbilt's support away. The death of a porter at the London School of Economics makes the public financing of an additional program at Keele somewhat harder to secure.

Economists have a complex term for this everyday phenomenon—as they do for almost everything else. When something happens in one place which causes damage and harm elsewhere, they call this an "external diseconomy." These are often used as arguments for governmental policy aimed at interfering with the free play of market forces. Proposals involve modifying the conditions of choice so that the "externalities are internalized." Hence, we find suggestions that the oil-drilling firms be taxed because they occasionally pollute California beaches. The actions of the offshore drillers may impose external costs on others, and the argument runs that they should be made fully liable for the damages. We shall certainly not discuss the technical economic theory of externalities here. Nonetheless, the relevance of this subject to the university setting is obvious. The effects which the unrest on one campus exerts on campuses everywhere cannot be hailed as beneficial. It is as if the strictly localized costs of disruption are magnified many times over in their impact on the university's image in society. Internalizing the full costs of localized trouble would require that the faculty-administration decision-maker add extra dimensions to his own subjective loss or damage estimate.

This provides us with a way of looking at a meaningful definition of responsibility in the current university turmoil. As administration and faculty leaders have made concession after concession to terrorists' demands, critics have often charged that their behavior was irresponsible. What could they mean? Perhaps these critics, and the public generally, intuitively imply that responsible behavior would reckon all costs, whether these be localized or whether they be spillover damages to the world at large.

As economists, we should predict that university authorities, or anyone else, would not worry about costs imposed on the world at large. To insure responsible (that is, full cost-recognizing) behavior, the conditions of choice would have to be changed so as to make these costs (or offsetting benefits) internal to the decision makers. Our task is analysis and prediction. Yet in passing we may allow our imagination to roam a bit by proposing schemes that illustrate operative principles. Imagine the trade association of university professors, the AAUP in the United States or its equivalent elsewhere, collecting extraordinary dues from its members to finance a set of university Peace Prizes. These would be awarded personally to those university and college presidents who succeed in maintaining peace with dignity. This scheme may not be so farfetched after all, especially if the AAUP be replaced by some wealthy donor. And, if we may offer a bit of advice to donors here, there might be worse ways of giving a dime. University

Peace Prizes would, at the very least, exert their efforts in the proper direction. Much current donor support does just the opposite.

While we are dreaming, let us suppose that the Ford Foundation had established, in 1960, such a set of prizes. If the foundation had devoted only one-tenth of its university-college support to these prizes during the decade of the 1960's, the beneficial effects to American higher education could easily have dwarfed all other programs—those of Ford and all the rest. Is it yet too late?


## Response within Rules

Universities are gradually beginning to cope with the terror that threatens them. Faculties and administrations are, day-by-day, learning that unrest is not going to cease and desist. Fewer and fewer are those who choose to behave like ostriches, to put their heads in the sands (or in the clouds), and refuse to get excited although the house is burning down. Experience is forcing a general recognition that the activists have discovered and are exploiting a new resource —terror. They have found this to be highly-productive virgin territory. As we have seen, they have been delicately tapping this new resource, always careful to shelter themselves as much as possible within the system's natural network of threshold-sensitivities. Their advances have been amazingly successful, considering that they have penetrated our world so deeply with hardly any (provoked) setbacks to their cause. However, the attitude that expects the terrorists to fold their tents and silently steal away (one which has been cunningly cultivated for so long) is beginning to be exposed as the height of folly.

Nonetheless, even to this date, few university authorities have learned the first lesson of response. Terror is not reduced by increasing its productivity to the terrorists. "Appeasement" has been discussed for so long by so many that any further elaboration is unnecessary. What is perhaps surprising is that our experience with Hitler in the 1930's is so often cited as proof of the theorem that appeasement does not pay. But quite apart from Hitler, and long before this tragic turn in human history was taken, elementary economics could have been used to provide the proof required. As we noted earlier, we do not reduce the excess demand for apples or automobiles by reducing their prices. That would only make eating or driving them more desirable than before. The self-equilibrating response is just the opposite. And the direction of response is vital in determining whether or not the whole interaction between those who demand and those who respond is self-correcting or destructively explosive. Predictions of rational conduct should be discounted for madmen. But with university terrorists, appeasement and concession makes no sense at all. These are no madmen. They are rational human beings who seek quite specific things and who have found a new means of accomplishing what they want at relatively little, if any, cost to themselves.

A parallel may be found in the Vietnam war strategy. Throughout the world, faculties and administrations have behaved in the face of student terror much as the United States behaved in Vietnam between 1963 and 1968, and with almost identical results. Confronted with terror, the response of the immensely stronger power has been deliberately restrained in the fear that more effective reaction would trigger escalation. Observing this quavering unwillingness of their more powerful opponent to respond in strength, the terrorists rush in, no longer like fools, and exploit their advantages through one-sided escalation. This has been the process through which faculties and administrations have been led into one agonizing reappraisal after another, with the cycle of terror and response gradually degenerating into what we see.

Here the parallel must stop, however. A reduction in United States involvement in Vietnam clearly remains a possible alternative. But for the university authorities "withdrawal" into oblivion is not a viable course. At some stage, and soon, the first lesson of response will be learned, and university authorities will take measures that will attempt to turn events toward equilibrium by reducing the profitability of terror. Evidence for this prediction is beginning to be seen everywhere. It is equally essential to recognize that, whenever effective university response is forthcoming, it will necessarily be governed by existing rules and regulations, written and unwritten. The constitutional structure of the university cannot be changed overnight. The university administrative official or faculty committee member, faced with the urgency of campus unrest, and fully cognizant of the first lesson in the strategy of response, must operate within the constraints that the university's structure imposes on him. These day-to-day operational choices, made within an existing set of rules and procedures, have to be separated from those deliberations and decisions that look toward longer-range reforms through changes in the basic rules themselves.

# The Just and the Unjust

When, as, and if university authorities begin to respond to terror, as we predict they must, one fact deserves special mention. The innocent will suffer along with the guilty in any effective restraints on student-faculty militancy. There *is* no other way. Regardless of political consequences, Governor Ronald Reagan invokes the impossible when he calls for an isolation of the rebellious few while preserving for the passive many all of the freedoms that they previously enjoyed. The predicted response must involve the identification, trial, and punishment of the few who generate the terror. But even if this response be forthcoming with diligence and courage by university authorities, they must in the process impose major costs on the many who deserve to be left alone.

These are external costs that are of a different kind from those we discussed earlier. The few who create chaos indirectly impose burdens on those who value freedom and tranquility. Traditionally, the university has been a community where faculty and student members alike enjoy almost maximal liberty so long as very broad tolerance limits are not abused. Throughout the years, academia has been a haven for the personal eccentrics, the oddballs, the kooks. This, in fact, has been one of its major attractions to those who value personal idiosyncrasy highly. Even for those who do not individually behave much differently from the man who punches a time clock, the option to order their own lives as they please has great value.

These values will be seriously undermined as a result of any attempt to deal with student-faculty activism, disruption, and terror. Authorities will respond, and in so doing they must impose on all explicit rules that are more restrictive than those previously in existence. The restoration of university-college order may come after the chaos, but such order cannot be accompanied by the relaxed and delightful nonchalance of days gone by. Examples are too numerous to count, but a few will probably suffice to make the point clear. Throughout its century and a half of experience, the University of Virginia allowed all students, undergraduate and graduate alike, free access to all library stacks and imposed no door checks in its libraries. Students remained honor-bound to respect the rules for borrowing books. In 1968, all this was suddenly changed. Door checks were introduced because book "losses" had become too high. Those few whose behavior flouted the long-standing tradition had imposed severe costs on all library users.

## Prediction and Prophecy

At San Francisco State College during the academic year 1968–1969, a long-neglected California law allowed state college authorities to respond to a minority faculty strike. Unauthorized absences from classroom duties for more than five days provided grounds for dismissal. The response was effective in imposing discipline on the militants, but in dusting off this old law to apply to the few, many faculty members who did not strike were made to feel that their own long-cherished freedom of action was diminished. And so it was. This new restriction, because it was directly imposed by the authorities, was cleverly exploited by the minority whose actions were indirectly responsible. In the process, the activists secured the unthinking support of many of those upon whom their own behavior had imposed severe costs.

The simple fact of response discussed here will not be welcomed by the nonactivist students and the nonactivist faculty members. Given the rules within which they must operate, university authorities will have to restrict the freedoms of all in order to impose discipline on the irresponsible. This is a cost that the responsible nonactivists must bear. No one likes to carry around an identity card in order to secure entrance to his university or college. Yet we shall probably all be forced to wear such badges in order that those who would destroy the structure can be effectively isolated and identified.

# Constitutional Change

It is relatively easy to predict how university decision-makers will respond to disruption in the immediate short-run context and within existing rules. It is much more difficult to project the shape of long-range changes in the constitutional structure of the university. Such changes may arise from different sources. Limited adjustment can be expected to arise from the internal deliberations of faculties. More significant modifications can be predicted in the form of additional constraints imposed externally by university governing boards. For state-financed universities and colleges, legislatures may directly lay down different rules and indirectly exert budgetary controls. Finally, and perhaps most hopefully, genuine innovations in university organization may well emerge from the establishment of new units.

## Faculty Initiative

Our analysis of university structure tells us something about predicted constitutional change. The success of the revolutionary minority in disrupting university life is directly traceable to the failure of the university to respond to the demands of student-consumers on the one hand and to those of the taxpayer-owners on the other. Pressures for fundamental changes in the rules governing university operation arise from these groups who are dissatisfied. This suggests that the major barrier to internally generated constitutional change will be that posed by faculties. If the university structure is to be modified so as to make it more responsive to the interest of students and taxpayers, the monopoly control of faculties and administrations must be reduced and perhaps dramatically. As the university is now organized, faculties make their own rules. Self-interest, therefore, will naturally prevent any constitutional revision that significantly reduces faculty power. For this reason, we can predict with reasonable accuracy that internal constitutional change in the university will be both limited in scope and tardy in coming.

As pressures mount, however, faculties will increasingly sense their precarious constitutional position. Realizing this, while at the same time seeking to preserve, if at all possible, their own ultimate powers of control and fearing external political intervention more than revolutionary terror, faculties may adopt rules changes that will create more chaos rather than its opposite. Currently, demands for student participation seem to be taken quite seriously by faculties everywhere. As we have indicated, however, the faculty response seems to be overtly biased toward meeting the demands of the terrorist innovators rather than toward plausible rules changes designed to incorporate limited and responsible student controls over program and instructional content.

We simply do not have sufficient faith in the wisdom of academic faculties to expect them to put their own house in order through dramatic internally generated constitutional change. This is despite our view that such changes would be in the enlightened and long-range self-interest of academicians everywhere. The majority of almost every university faculty will oppose changes that will introduce indirect student-consumer controls through interuniversity competition. Faculty and administration behavior seems almost expressly designed so as to go on inviting the imposition of additional external constraints. One single example is perhaps sufficient. In a virtuoso demonstration of stupidity, those same faculty leaders who most vociferously opposed tuition charges at the University of California in 1966 were also the most vocal in their opposition to the university regents' interference with "academic affairs" in 1968.

As they have behaved in the whole sorry show, and as we should expect them to continue to behave, faculties "play" to the wrong audience. As intellectuals, faculty members have been lulled into believing their own myths. Somehow, and strangely at that, they have become convinced that their group alone sets standards of taste, style, and public opinion. This has produced the closed circle in which their whole efforts seem aimed to please only their own kind. They have acted as if theirs is a world apart, that the freely-floating island truly exists. The rabble outside is somehow duty-bound to provide the manna, and he who so much as questions the one-way relationship is deemed a philistine. The academic play, of course, cannot be performed for the players only. But who would be brave enough to predict that faculties have yet learned this lesson?

# Prediction and Prophecy

## Governing Boards' Initiative

Formally, modern universities are owned not by faculties but by those governing boards that serve as agents for taxpayers or contributors. If faculties cannot be expected to adopt the constitutional changes that will produce viability in confrontation, what can we say about governing boards?

Empirical evidence lends support to a simple first prediction here. Governing boards are taking, and will continue to take, an increasingly active role in university control—whether this be in the day-to-day operation of facilities or in laying down changes in rules and regulations. The failure of faculties and administrations to restore effective order in the face of violence necessarily requires that governing boards act in the breach. But how will they act? This is a more difficult question. Nevertheless, a few general predictions may be advanced. Membership on university and college governing boards is not a profession, and individual members are not necessarily experts in governance of universities or of anything else. They cannot and do not devote their full time to their higher educational responsibilities. They are not, and cannot be, sensitive to the subtle nuances of the academic milieu. The blunderbuss rather than the stiletto provides the appropriate metaphor for any imposition of constraints on university activities.

It is almost inevitable, therefore, that some of the actions taken by governing boards, and especially in the current setting, will accomplish precisely the opposite of that which is intended. Some of the attempts at imposing new constraints will fan, not quench, the flames of chaos. Conversely, it is almost equally inevitable that some of the actions taken will prove to be highly productive. Some steps will be taken which may, with a bit of luck, stop terror in its tracks. Where these are tried, especially where the necessary legislative framework is first established, within a few short years the chaos of the 1960's may become a relic in history.

In the current pattern of university organization, the actions of governing boards in the early 1970's may provide the critical testing grounds for institutional viability. More than anyone, or anywhere else in the current setting, governing boards will determine whether or not specific institutions will be plunged further into chaos or whether a new normalcy will soon be restored. We have predicted that faculties will not put their own houses in order. This was a generalized prediction for all universities and colleges. (Personally, we would relish having to eat crow in the dining hall at Berkeley in 1975.) We are prepared to make no such general prediction with respect to the behavior of external governing boards. These are made up of men whose self-interest is not closely or directly tied to the existing university organization as such. Indeed, the absence of such a conflict of interest provides the rationale for the very existence of these boards. There is no simple basis for prediction, therefore, as to how the men who make them up will behave individually or collectively as they are forced, almost willy-nilly, to concern themselves more and more with university affairs. Furthermore, there is no professional association of regents, trustees, governors, and so forth, no formal or informal organization that either sets common value standards or from which such standards emerge as a natural course of events. There is no "party line" for members of university and college boards. The regents of the University of California may behave in a way that is totally different from that of the board of visitors of Virginia Polytechnic Institute.

Prediction, then, is limited to saying that the responses of governing boards will be varied from one university to another. This implies that the results will also exhibit wide variations. The actions of some boards will, without doubt, help to accelerate the destruction process. Conversely, other boards may be highly successful. Universities that are fortunate enough to have such governing boards will emerge as the leaders in the academic world of the 1970's. But the volatility of such leadership in face of the current turmoil should be recognized. In the university world where change, if at all apparent, was evolutionary, traditions of leadership were difficult both to establish and to destroy. In the new world where change is revolutionary, the reputation of decades can be destroyed within weeks. As the unrest mounts and spreads, however, leadership opportunities will automatically be opened for those institutions which, for whatever reasons, succeed in maintaining scholarship with decorum. As the grotesque fantasy of yesterday becomes the reality of today, universities may soon begin to secure positions of leadership by comparative scorecards. "No riots this year" and "no obeisance to militant demands" might then be included among the hallmarks of excellence.

We have not discussed the predicted response of legislatures. In the confused legal framework as it stands, in the United States and elsewhere, some university administrations that have attempted to take direct action against disruptive student activism have been challenged in the courts. They have been prevented from effectively containing terror on their campuses by court rulings based on the familiar principles of due process and free speech. New legislation may be predicted that is aimed at facilitating the responsiveness of university authorities to growing violence and terror. This will probably allow them greater freedom to enforce discipline. The simple idea that even students must be responsible to the law of the land may be re-established. Indeed, this seemed to be the primary legislative response to events in California in 1969. It seems also probable that the people, through their legislatures, will take some steps toward curtailing the availability of funds going to higher education, or, if not actual curtailment, at least some retardation in the rate of increase. As enormous sums of taxpayers' hard-earned money seem to subsidize more and more disruptive student activism, universities will surely begin to suffer serious budgetary problems stemming from some such "backlash" effect. Would it be surprising if, say, in Wisconsin, where 66 cents out of every dollar of the State budget is spent on education (and where student disruption has reached some of its loftiest peaks) legislatures were to cut down on this kind of expenditure? We are not predicting that legislatures will necessarily "panic," and withdraw financial support overnight. It stands to reason however, that they will be taking an increasingly dim view in practice of the growing student anarchy. And, in this respect as elsewhere, those who have not abused the public's trust will be forced to suffer deprivation along with the abusers.

As with governing boards, the responses of legislatures to the chaos in the universities and colleges will not be uniform. Some legislatures will probably rush in with ill-conceived and punitive measures that will accelerate campus disruption and/or destruction. Other legislative bodies may provide the guidelines that governing boards and administrations require to set things right. A general infusion of the view that legislatures can and will act through the control and allocation of public funds might work wonders on faculty-administration spirit.

With legislative action, as with the action of the revolutionaries, there are important spillover effects. American state legislatures, in particular, tend to act similarly. Strong legislative reaction to university unrest in California, for example, will surely make it easier for similar reaction to take place in Oregon or Idaho. Something of the domino theory applies in both directions here. As more and more universities succumb to the terror, the activists find it easier to capture those remaining immune from unrest. But, if and when the tide is turned, by faculties and administrations, by governing boards, or by legislatures, the fallen dominoes will rise in sequence. Re-establishment of order in Berkeley, London or Columbia will surely make it easier, not harder, to re-establish order in Madison.

## Toward the Heliopolis of the 1970's?

Sophocles' *Oedipus Rex* and Aeschylus' *Agamemnon* provide examples of the excesses of men which often precede disaster—no less in the lives of their institutions than in their personal worlds. Macbeth, Lear, or Othello also bear testimony to man's external fear of hubris. Yet neither man nor his institutions ever seem to learn. Today, it is as if Nemesis had once again struck; as if academe is being punished for its wrongdoings over many a decade.

Perhaps, as we have seen, the fortunes and misfortunes of our world will be equalized within its own existing constitutional structure. It may be that academia will in the last analysis pull itself up by its own bootstraps, thanks to its internal institutional resilience. On the other hand, the university world as we have known it may be doomed to die. Even this, however, might take place in order that the eternal flame of scholarship may live. If, in fact, as the Phoenix built its nest within which to die, the academe should also perish in the chaos it has so diligently manufactured for itself, there may still be hope. Pliny, we may recall, maintained that a worm of the dead bird's body would evolve into a new and greater Phoenix. So perhaps a new era may also turn the death knells of our contemporary university world into some equally resplendent golden creature with red feathers—this time in our academic Heliopolis of the 1970's. Whether or not we wish to distinguish novel ways of making old goods from old ways of making novelties, it may be that the ever-mounting problems of the academic world are gradually making way for the creative response of the modern innovator.

In prehistoric times most inventions or discoveries were stumbled upon by sheer accident. With the development of civilization, however, man's ingenuity and natural impulse toward innovation and change gradually ranged into the realms of pure thought and research—inspired, more often than not, by pressing problems or hidden opportunities arising from his environment. Is it not reasonable to expect, therefore, that as today's chaos in the university world deepens, conditions may also be developing which will lead us to respond more constructively and more creatively to the many difficulties which surround us?

While there is a minority in our midst who will probably accept no possible adjustment of the present system, is there not an alternative approach to student anarchism? It has been said that to stand flat-footed waiting for one's opponent to strike is no way to carry on either serious or sporting affairs. Assuming, therefore, that the university authorities will at some point satiate their recently acquired taste for masochism, what additional institutional developments could we predict in the overall university scene? What new forms of organization could be expected to arise?

Perhaps the first major innovation will be anarchist centers of learning (such as already exist in Germany, France, and elsewhere), where all those who reject the very principles of "orthodox" university life (whatever these may become with the passage of time) will concentrate. Several good reasons come to mind in support of this expectation. Anarchist universities might be established to provide a constructive challenge to the many talented, but implacable, enemies both of the presently instituted academic system and of its constitutionally controlled processes of change and modernization. Should such institutions exist, every student who decides to pursue a higher education would naturally have a new option. He could either join an anarchist university or, before being admitted to a conventional university, he could provide a solemn promise that he would abide by its rules and regulations—its constitution. The explicit understanding would follow that if he did not honor his pledge a place would no longer be available for him. Making such a choice possible to potential and actual students might well be in the interests both of the taxpayer and the existing university authorities, in which case the financing of such anarchist centers might prove less difficult than would appear at first glance. A substantial net gain to society might, in fact, emerge by adding such a new dimension of freedom to the process of education. Furthermore, the argument is strengthened by the possible long-term educational and sociological advantages of such possible anarchist experiments. Finally, there would accrue some obvious savings in damage and other more general (private and social) wastage that is rampant in today's academic world.

As Bernard Scott has suggested, we should expect that the educational activities of these anarchist centers would not immediately reach the highest academic standards. But it would be informative to see how things settle down, especially through the eyes of sufficiently gifted social psychologists and social anthropologists. The opportunity would arise for assessing what, if any, could be the benefits to society for taking seriously these novel views on educational organization. Experience from small tutorial groups suggests that the collective activities of a learning-group can often be of some value to all concerned. The anarchist centers could possibly provide useful data, therefore, on this kind of voluntary-collective student self-help. What is more, it is not altogether unreasonable to expect that the students might be more acceptable to their fellowmen when they ultimately leave these anarchist centers than upon admission to them.

One would expect, of course, that such anarchist institutions would function independently of the rest of the academic system. Quite apart from the cost attached to setting up experimental units within existing high-cost university structures, common sense suggests that it would be difficult to run either if anarchist and conventional universities should exist side by side on the same campus. Spatial dispersion might be essential for a useful and worthwhile comparison between conventional academic wisdom and futuristic methods involving such total lack of authority, ex-

aminations, discrimination for entry, accreditation processes, and so forth.

The general trend toward anarchist organization is to
some extent already apparent, but with one notable exception. The "new wave" has been allowed to manifest itself *within* existing universities. How wise this strategy
can be, only time will show. Many institutions of higher
learning are already facing roughly this kind of competition
within their own borders. Student-run mini-colleges,
with their own special course offerings, are everywhere
springing up on university campuses. Known as experimental
colleges or free universities, these schools-within-schools
have already won varying acceptance from university administrations. The total number of such student-organized
projects across the Western world is, of course, difficult to
determine. But they multiplied rapidly over the decade of
the 1960's, and they appear to be more than a fad. In these
experimental units emphasis invariably falls on group discussion and student-devised and student-led learning tech-
niques in lieu of the more usual lecture-oriented presenta-
tions by duly accredited professors.

Where can this lead? Will the parent universities benefit
as a result? It is difficult to tell. But one thing is certain.
The whole tradition of the more conventional organizational
forms for the dissemination and development of wisdom
will be practically questioned. Conventional universities
may gradually move more toward self-education, based on
"strong interaction," group discussion, informal settings, no
grades, and other "laboratory" aspects of these "standard"

experimental schemes. It may even be that the latter will "prove" to be alternative, and more effective, ways of getting everyone motivated than through the "imposed motivation" that conventional Western ways apparently suggest. For the time being, of course, only a few colleges have formally managed to partake in this great intellectual "feast of the future." For example, in Oberlin College, Ohio, the administration has already granted credit to student-organized courses on the above lines, including black intellectual thought and contemporary black life. In proper style, too, this sudden gust of enlightenment has been occasioned by the one and only legitimate form of imposed motivation— that of student violence and terror which these days must precede all leaps ahead in the process of learning.

But when all is said and done, perhaps it is time to stop fooling ourselves. For there really remains but one source of solid common sense upon which the entire future of the academic world is likely to be based—if it is to survive at all. This source is the vast majority of men and women in university life who, in their varied and fundamental pursuits, are after all no different from those in every other walk of life. As Howard Ferns has explained, young people in the university world are no less interested in money, prestige, promotion, opportunities, and security than any other group of people. They compete for resources as much as business men do; and, when resources are scarce, they are as fierce and conservative (as opposed to being "wasteful") as any other breed. It follows that if their considerable intelligence and energy were spent directly in satisfying the demand for higher education, and in inventing ways of selling their products to an ever-widening and equally well-endowed body of student-customers, everyone would certainly benefit as a result. Does it not follow that some shift in this direction can be predicted? As the chaos spreads, as the current structure of universities suffers further damage, as the rational, hardworking, and purposeful majority of students becomes increasingly tormented, the deeply felt need for different, legitimate, truly superior methods and purposes for higher education will have to supersede the ugliness of our status quo. Can it be long before the modern innovator will "strike," exposing once and for all the built-in nonsense of a system that has failed to recognize that students everywhere would much prefer to buy better things than to get lesser goods free; or that faculties might prefer to sell worthwhile goods as opposed to being subsidized in wasting scarce resources? Would it not be evident, too, that taxpayers' problems of control largely vanish in such a scheme of things?

The record may in the end be put right. The private innovators, the Fords of academia, should certainly emerge to create their own independent universities. In so doing they will tap the powers of competitive or market-oriented behavior. And can they not be predicted to become the successful trailbreakers in the education industry? Putting it alternatively, would it be surprising if the successful universities which emerge should be those which put maximum emphasis on satisfying the customer and the community? As Harry Johnson has argued, these universities would

relatively uninformed buyers of the product, parents or students, could not have sensed the differentiation of the product—at any rate certainly not immediately. All of this would have been true even in a world of purely private, full tuition-charging universities. The problem facing the innovator would have been compounded many times over in a setting dominated by tuition-free, state-financed universities and colleges. Here, the degree of differentiation in product would indeed have had to seem immense to the prospective purchaser to induce much switch of custom.

Much of this has changed, in favor of the innovator, in the disruptive 1960's. More and more faculty members may be willing, indeed eager, to accept employment in institutions that offer stability and security to life and property. The turmoil may have become an important nonpecuniary disadvantage of the disturbed monolithic institutions, and faculty personnel may now accept even salary cuts in order to insure tranquility in their freedom to pursue their scholarly objectives. The cost disadvantage that faced the prospective innovator in the 1950's may have already been reversed by the events of the 1960's. But the shifts on the side of the buyers of the product are perhaps even more significant. As existing institutions come to be more and more vulnerable to overt acts of terror involving physical destruction of property and danger to life itself, the prospective buyers of higher education will sense, and probably acutely so, the difference between the product offered by existing institutions and one that can convincingly offer study-amid-stability. The shift in the terms-of-trade in favor of the innovator will become even more pronounced if taxpayer support of existing university systems should wane.

These are our private predictions and prophecies. They are the shapes of the academic future that we discern. The massive university monolith, dominated by hidebound faculty rigidity, is not among them. This Clark Kerr monstrosity goes the way of the dinosaur. The violence and terror we see are perhaps the catalysts for its demise. A few such structures will no doubt survive, even until such times as they can be labelled "prehistoric". Elementary skills and a little good fortune could see to this. But for the others, the intellectual ghetto lies just ahead. More and more, they will be deserted by the responsible students, by the respectable faculty members, and by the rational taxpayers. When history strikes the balance sheet, something akin to Nero's infamous last words as he stabbed himself to death may be heard again: "What an artist dies in me!" In the modern academic pandemonium of absurd violence, terror, and obeisance this may have also been the perishing wail of the universities we have known. That which rises from the ashes may, once again, be the most splendid edifice of all.

> *. . . it is a general rule of human nature that people despise those who treat them well and look up to those who make no concessions.*
> Thucydides, *The Peloponnesian War*

# Selected Bibliography

Alchian, Armen A. "The Economic and Social Impact of Free Tuition." *The New Individualist Review* (Winter, 1968), pp. 42–58.

———. "Private Property and the Relative Cost of Tenure." In *The Public Stake in Union Power*, edited by Philip D. Bradley. Charlottesville: University of Virginia Press, 1959.

———. *Pricing and Society*. London: The Institute of Economic Affairs, 1967.

Alchian, Armen A. and Allen, William R. *University Economics*. 2nd ed. Belmont, Calif.: Wadsworth Press, 1967.

———. "What Price Zero Tuition?" *Michigan Quarterly Review* (October, 1968), pp. 269–272.

Becker, Gary. *Human Capital*. New York: Columbia University Press, 1964.

Blaug, Mark. "The Rate of Return on Investment in Education in Great Britain." *The Manchester School* (September, 1965).

# Selected Bibliography

Buchanan, James M. "Student Revolts, Academic Liberalism, and Constitutional Attitudes." *Social Research,* XXXV (Winter, 1966), 666–680.

Burns, Joseph M. and Chiswick, Barry R. "An Economic Analysis of State Support for University Education." *Western Economic Journal,* VII (March, 1969), 84–95.

Devletoglou, Nicos E. "The Berkeley Syndrome." *Encounter,* XXXIII (August, 1969), 96–97.

Ferns, H. S. *Towards an Independent University.* London: Institute of Economic Affairs, 1968.

Friedman, Milton. *Capitalism and Freedom.* Chicago: University of Chicago Press, 1962.

———. "The Role of Government in Education." In *Economics and Public Interest,* edited by R. A. Solo. New Brunswick: Rutgers University Press, 1955.

Harris, S. E., ed. *Higher Education in the United States.* Cambridge: Harvard University Press, 1960.

Hook, Sidney. *Academic Freedom and Academic Anarchy.* Boulder: University of Colorado Press, 1968.

Jencks, Christopher and Riesman, David. *The Academic Revolution.* New York: Doubleday, 1966.

Johnson, Harry G. "The Economics of Student Protest." *New Society,* November 7, 1968, pp. 673–675.

———. "An Economist Looks at Student Unrest." *The Sunday Telegraph,* December 1, 1968.

Letwin, William. "Dangers of Reform: The Case of English Universities." Mimeographed. London: The London School of Economics.

Lipset, Seymour M. "American Student Activism." Rand Corporation, P–3893, July, 1968, p. 44.

———. "The Possible Effects of Student Activism on International Relations." Rand Corporation, P–3943, September, 1968, p. 40.

# Selected Bibliography

Prest, A. R. *Financing University Education*. London: The Institute of Economic Affairs, 1966.

Scott, Bernard. "The Free University of Stanford?" *University Quarterly*, September, 1968, pp. 439–442.

Tullock, Gordon. "Information Without Profit." In *Papers in Non-Market Decision Making*, I, edited by G. Tullock. Charlottesville, Va.: Thomas Jefferson Center for Political Economy, 1966.

———. *The Politics of Bureaucracy*. Washington: The Public Affairs Press, 1963.

Vickrey, W. S. "A Proposal for Financing Higher Education." In *The Economics of Higher Education*, edited by S. J. Mushkin. Washington, D. C.: U. S. Government Printing Office, 1962.

West, E. G. *Education and the State: A Study in Political Economy*. London: Institute of Economic Affairs, 1965.

Wiseman, J. and Peacock, A. T. *Education for Democrats*. London: The Institute of Economic Affairs, 1964.

# Index

# Index

Columbia University, student revolt, 128, 168

community of scholars, 54, 62, 63

competition, among universities, 30, 32–33, 58, 59, 145–146, 151, 173–175, 175–176

congestion, vs. rationing, in universities, 19–20, 21

constitutional reform, of universities, 156–157, 160, 168

consumer preferences, and product quality, 39–40

consumer sovereignty, 145

Cornell University, student revolt, 80

cost-benefit analysis, of terrorism, 135

creeping reform, of universities, 134, 138–140, 142

demand, and price of university education, 8, 18–19, 32

democracy, participatory, 146, 148; vs. student terrorism, 103–105, 142, 143; and university chaos, 4; in university faculties, 53–56

democratization, of universities, 143–144, 146, 147

economic analysis, 4, 5, 6, 8, 9, 10, 15, 34–35, 89, 90, 100–101, 102, 135, 150, 154; of academic tenure, 48–50; cost-benefit calculus, 130–131; costs of race guilt complex, 129–130; external diseconomy, 152–154; of faculty democracy, 54–56; of interuniversity competition, 56–60, 173–175; of student majority vs. activists, 125–127; of university ownership, 85–86; of value of university education, 67–70, 71–

73; of violence, 4, 5, 96, 112, 115–120, 125–127, 130–131

economic good, 6–7, 20

enrollments, university, 18, 97–98

Era of Neolatry, 147, 149

ethical rules, and violence, 123

ethnic minorities, and university admission, 42, 93

Europe, university competition in, 58, 59; university systems, 62

exchange, vs. sex and violence, 113–115

experimental colleges, 172–173

external diseconomy, and universities, 152–154

faculties: academic tenure, 48–50; conservatism of, 47; control of quality of product, 7, 8–9, 39–40, 46; control of student numbers, 41, 43–46; control of universities, 15, 52, 53–56, 59–60, 76–77, 100–101; domination by academic liberals, 130; interuniversity competition, 56–58; pay scales, 7, 31, 51–52, 175, 176; as producers of education, 8–9, 35; race guilt complex, 128–130; research and publication, 7, 106–107; selection of preferred consumers, 36–37, 41, 42, 43; selection of preferred output, 38–39; vs. student activism, 50, 51–52, 77–80, 101–102, 103, 118–120, 154; undergraduate teaching, 106–108; university ownership, 83; university reform, 160–162, 163, 167, 175, 176, 177; *see also* academic liberals

Fechner, Gustav, 132

feedback, from consumers, 8, 39–40, 43, 46

Ferns, Howard S., 173

# Index

# Index

O'Neill, Eugene, 34
Orwell, George, 54, 119
ownership, of universities, 65–66, 81–84, 85–86, 118, 123, 163
Oxford University, tutorial system, 43

parents, as buyers of education, 14, 77–78, 151
Paris, number of students, 98; student revolt, 138, 142, 149
Parsons College, 46
participatory democracy, 146, 148
*Peloponnesian War*, quoted, 177
permissiveness, and student terrorism, 144–145; and university education, 14
Plato, 146; quoted, 15–16
political issues, and university chaos, 4
politicization, of universities, 49–50, 64
population explosion, 14
price, of university education, vs. demand-supply, 18–19, 32
pricing, and selection of consumers, 37–38; and university admission, 22–23
*Pricing and Society*, 60–61
private universities, and student unrest, 79–80
professional training, vs. education, 10–11, 13
public, and university chaos, 3

quality, of university education, 7, 8, 9, 18–19, 31, 46–47, 98–99, 151, 161; producer vs. consumer control of, 39–40

race guilt complex, 128–130
rationing, 19–20, 21, 31, 94; under price system, 37–38; and special

groups of students, 26, 42, 93; of zero-price product, 36, 41, 42
Reagan, Ronald, 23, 157
religious conversion, and university education, 13
rents, and faculty salaries, 31
Ridgeway, James, 66
Riesman, David, 92
Rollenberg, Simon, 116
Rome, student unrest, 142
Rousseau, J. J., 35

San Francisco State College, faculty discipline, 159; student revolt, 64, 125
scarcity value, of university education, 20–21
science, and academic independence, 63–64
Scott, Bernard, 171
secondary schools, terrorism in, 144
self-equilibrating response, to terrorism, 154–156
sex, vs. exchange and violence, 113-115
Shakespeare, 86, 147
Smith, Adam, 51
social issues, and university chaos, 4
state, and free university tuition, 7; and university ownership, 84
student organized courses, 173
students: activism, 3, 4, 99–100, 105, 135; admission criteria, 26, 30, 41–43, 56; apathy of majority, 105–106, 107, 110–111, 125–127; attitudes of, and free tuition, 27–29; attitudes toward activism, 110–111; availability for activism, 108–110; as beneficiaries of special subsidy, 21–22, 23–24; causes of activism, 95–99; as child-men, 13–15, 95;

184

# Index